111

Fabulous Food Finds

Best Bites in the Bluegrass

by

David Dominé

Cover design and book layout by Asher Graphics
Front cover photos by James Asher
Photos on back cover, endsheets and inside pages by
David Dominé unless otherwise credited.

Manufactured in the United States of America

All book order correspondence should be addressed to:

McClanahan Publishing House, Inc.
P.O. Box 100
Kuttawa, KY 42055

800-544-6959

www.kybooks.com

Hand-made by Ron and Jane Harris in Louisville, Happy Balls
are a fabulous food find for chocolate lovers everywhere.

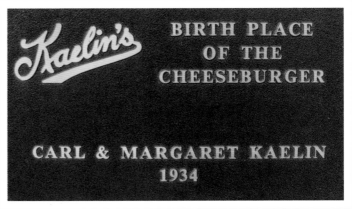

We are reminded of Kentucky's fabulous food history all
across the Commonwealth.

For

Ramon Garcia

A faithful sidekick and driver
on so many of my culinary adventures

Preface

What is a fabulous food find? Although the term seems self-explanatory, some might find themselves wondering how a location merits inclusion in this book of Fabulous Food Finds. First, let me start by saying that this is not meant to be a listing of Kentucky's best restaurants and eating places but rather a cross section of those eateries that to my mind best represent the culinary traditions of the region, those that form a loose collection of the places that have stood out in some way or other as I've traveled throughout the state and sampled the fare on offer. Undoubtedly there are many wonderful restaurants that could have been included in this book, but only 111 of them made it, for a variety of reasons.

One explanation is the food, of course. Be it home cooking or haute cuisine, the fare at an eatery has to be just plain good, if not outstanding, to be considered a fabulous food find. But although what's on the menu does play an important part, it is not necessarily the determining factor — or even a primary factor — in an establishment's inclusion in this book. Also considered are the restaurant's location and history, for example. Is it housed in an old building or did something of importance happen there in the past? Another thing I look at is the longevity of the place, because if a diner or barbecue joint has been around for 50 years, chances are they're doing something right. In addition to that, I also think about the eatery's overall atmosphere, as well as its proximity to points of local interest, significance in the fabric of the community, and the people you meet there. And since this is meant to showcase the best tastes that all of Kentucky has to offer, from one end of the state to the other, I also tend to favor places that have been overlooked or those that might get you into unexplored regions. So all in all, a fabulous food find is the sum of its parts, an embodiment of the flavors, feels and foodstuffs that define the experience of eating out, wherever that experience may take you. So enjoy these *111 Fabulous Food Finds*, either in your armchair or your automobile, and savor the best bites in the Bluegrass.

A Word or Two of Advice

Restaurants are notorious for changing their days and hours of operation, so for that reason I suggest you always call ahead and confirm that a certain place is open before you pay them a visit — especially when the trip involves a long drive. There are two time zones in Kentucky and some counties are dry, so keep that in mind as well. In addition, menus change frequently, so if you're heading off to a certain locale for a certain dish, you might want to confirm it's still on the menu before you go. It's also good to find out if the restaurant is one of those that only takes cash or if it's in an area where people can still smoke in public places.

Apart from that, I find it's always best to keep an open mind when trying a new location. Instead of building up the expectation of a great meal, look forward to the experience itself and be prepared to take in the whole scene around you: the sights, smells, sounds, feelings — and of course, the flavors — that make a restaurant unique. Tastes are very personal, and often contingent on a number of factors, so just because I thought a specific eatery was a fabulous food find, it doesn't mean you will do the same.

One thing I can assure you of, however, is that the restaurants in this book represent the best and most interesting Kentucky has to offer, from one end of the Bluegrass to the other, and using this guide will help you experience the best bites out there, all the while getting to know the state better and appreciating it more. So, let *111 Fabulous Food Finds* be your companion as you explore the hamlets and back roads of Kentucky, but be adventuresome and let your stomach be your guide as you search out new favorites! Happy travels and happy eating from the Bluegrass Peasant!

Introduction

According to the Kentucky Chamber of Commerce, there are more than 10,000 eating places in the state, and its largest city, Louisville often appears at the very top of annual national lists for the highest per capita rate of people who eat out. So is it any wonder that people here love their restaurants? In short, Kentucky is a state of food lovers. From Paducah in the west to Pikeville in the east, from Covington in the north to Corbin in the south, there are roughly 5 million inhabitants, most of whom like to eat out.

One of these people who enjoys eating out, I have compiled this list of places to eat if you want to experience the culinary bounty that is Kentucky after years of traveling around the state in search of the perfect meal. From elegant eateries to diners and dives, from holes in the wall to hometown hideaways, from roadside restaurants to backwoods barbecues, *111 Fabulous Food Finds* showcases the best places to enjoy the best bites in the Bluegrass.

Be it country store, backwoods barbecue pit, burger joint, greasy spoon, neighborhood dive, main street diner, tavern, bakery, sweet shop or upscale restaurant, the Bluegrass State offers a great variety and number of ways to satisfy a hungry appetite.

However many eateries in Kentucky, such as Weaver's Hot Dogs in Corbin or Lexington's Parquette Drive-In, do more than just fulfill our taste cravings – they provide a nostalgic link to the past or connect us to the stories and individuals that shape our communities. Louisville's Oakroom and English Grill, both elegant hotel restaurants, nourish an aesthetic sense, a need for luxury, while some, like Granny's Kitchen in Russellville, bring people together. Others, like Holly Hill Inn in Midway, provide a creative outlet for the culinary talent that preserve or redefine kitchen traditions, and others – Rick's White Light Diner in Frankfort or Covington's Anchor Grill, for example – serve as a quirky home away from home or late night getaway. Many do all of these things, proving that a restaurant is often more than just a place to eat, while others, in fact, simply offer a no-frills setting where patrons can get a quick bite.

Whatever the reason you hit the road in search of Fabulous Food Finds, you're bound to get a good taste of Kentucky and discover the flavors that make it a unique culinary destination. So, grab your knife and fork and get ready to hit the road with the Bluegrass Peasant, because it's time to eat!

Acknowledgements

Iowe a huge debt of gratitude not only to all the people who steered me in the direction of Kentucky's Fabulous Food Finds, but also to writers Marty Godbey and Gary West, whose books about dining out across the state proved invaluable in carrying out the research for this project. I'd also like to thank Dixon Dedmann, Matt Willinger, Ben Gettinger and the team at Estes Public Relations who helped me round up missing information and last minute artwork before the book went to print. For the most part, I used my own pictures, but on the rare occasion I used professional photos, I give credit to the photographer in the book.

As with my last project, kudos to my proofing gremlins Wendy Demaree, Beth Schott, and Laura Horan for their help and to Jim Asher for his work laying out the book. Thanks as well to my publisher Michelle Stone, Jo Doty and the others at McClanahan who made this book a reality.

In addition, I'd also to like to thank Professor Gabriele Bosley, my friend, colleague and mentor at Bellarmine University for her continued encouragement, support and the role she has played in helping me obtain funding for my food-related projects in Kentucky and around the world. Thanks to the generous assistance from the International Programs Office at Bellarmine University over the years, I have been fortunate to carry out cultural and food research in Puerto Rico, the Dominican Republic, Belize, Guatemala, Costa Rica, Panama, El Salvador, Nicaragua, Honduras, Ecuador, Peru, Germany and Austria. Every time I come back from one of my trips, though, I do so with a renewed appreciation of the Fabulous Food Finds in Kentucky!

Contents

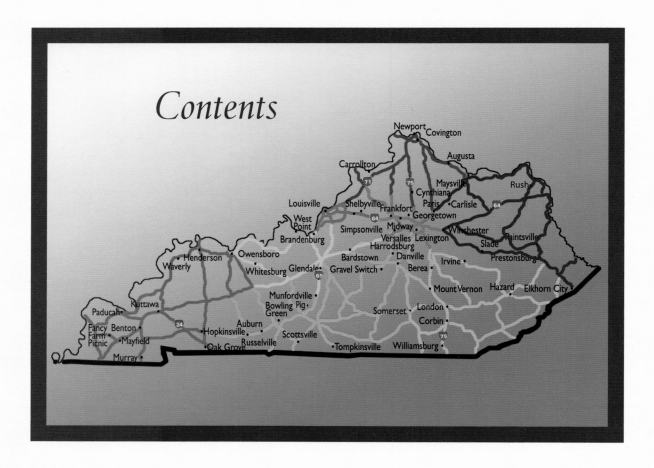

A historical marker in front of the recently demolished Masterson's Restaurant in Louisville commemorates the inventor of benedictine, another of Kentucky's Fabulous Food Finds.

610 Magnolia Avenue
Louisville, Kentucky 40208
(502) 636-0783

610 Magnolia

Located in a simple carriage house in the heart of historic Old Louisville, 610 Magnolia offers its guests an exceptional combination of southern hospitality and urban sophistication that earns it regular accolades from state and national press. The approach to food at 610 Magnolia is a simple one based on the farm-to-table agricultural movement and there is an emphasis on ever changing seasonal menus incorporating straightforward yet stylish preparations. With its rustic brick floors, wooden ceiling beams, mullioned windows and French doors opening onto an inviting garden patio, the interior of the restaurant is an uncomplicated statement in elegance. This sets the stage for a unique dining experience where guests sit at polished mahogany tables set with Frette linens and Riedel crystal while enjoying a New American cuisine with global influences and a preference for local organic products.

This is the vision of Edward Lee, a New York City native who began working in restaurants at the age of 14. Aside from cooking in several establishments in the newly built Trump Tower on 5th Avenue, Lee graduated magna cum laude with a degree in literature from New York University and he returned to the culinary world after a brief stint in publishing. During a visit to Louisville for the Derby, Lee was so impressed with the local restaurant scene and Kentucky's rich array of growers that he ultimately decided 610 Magnolia would be the perfect place to continue his culinary mission. Today, diners enjoy innovative selections that include creations like Kentucky fried duck with sweet potato polenta, and grilled sorghum quail with pumpkin seeds and roasted grapes for starters, and main courses such as wild boar chop with bourbon mustard and braised bacon Carolina rice, and Chesapeake striped bass with mussel risotto and broccoli rabe. Lee's menu is pre-fixed and allows guests the opportunity to choose between three, four and seven courses, with or without selected wine pairings. Dinner here's an elegant affair just steps from Old Louisville's St. James Court and that's what makes it one of Kentucky's Fabulous Food Finds.

In December 2010 610 Magnolia chef Ed Lee won on TV's Iron Chef.

Amon's Sugar Shack

3776 West Somerset
Somerset, Kentucky 42564
(606) 678-4392

If you're a morning person, Amon's Sugar Shack is a good place to get the day started in Somerset. It opens seven days a week at 5:00 a.m. and there's usually a car or two in the parking lot waiting to get first pick of the homemade baked goodies that have made the place famous. *Southern Living* magazine has written it up more than once and when it was named "Number One Food Find Across the South" in the baking category, it even beat out the famous Café du Monde in New Orleans. Although there are some 70 types of bakery items available at Amon's — these include pastries, brownies, bagels, muffins, cookies, breads, pies and custom-decorated cakes — the donuts have solidified its reputation as one of the state's culinary treasures. The raised donuts are yeasty and light as air, and the cake donuts are moist and flavorful; popular varieties include the plain glazed yeast donut, coconut cake donuts and cinnamon pinwheels.

Amon's got its start in 1951 when Amon Stephens and his wife Rosemary started a business delivering homemade doughnuts around town. Today it's still a family-run restaurant and chances are you'll find several generations working side by side in the kitchen or checking on guests out in the dining room. Although the baked goods are their biggest draw, Amon's serves a variety of items for breakfast and lunch as well. From-scratch biscuits and gravy are popular in the morning, and in the afternoons patrons crowd in for ham salad and pimento cheese sandwiches, among other standards. Although they've got lots of good things to start the day right, it's the donuts that makes Amon's Sugar Shack one of the many Fabulous Food Finds in Kentucky.

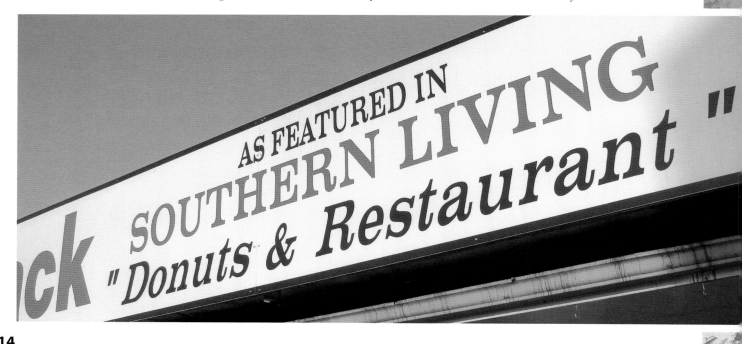

Anchor Grill

438 West Pike Street
Covington, Kentucky 41011
(859) 431-9498

The neon sign in the front window of Covington's Anchor Grill says it all: "We may doze, but never close." The famed motto has earned this quintessential greasy spoon a faithful clientele since it opened in 1946, and today the local landmark is known for its enjoyably kitschy atmosphere as much as it is for its short-order cooking. Gruff, unhurried waitresses that call you "honey," a shabby décor with a somewhat nautical theme, quirky patrons seemingly straight from the set of a David Lynch film — these are some of the things that mark the Anchor Grill experience.

But for the full effect, pop a quarter into the jukebox in the rear room and enjoy the show: bathed in colored lights, a half disco ball starts spinning on the ceiling as a corner diorama comes to life, featuring Barbie and a big band grooving to the beat. From the smoke-blurred sheen of the plexiglass stage, it's safe to assume that this eccentric ensemble has given its fair share of encore performances to the hungry crowds at the Anchor Grill.

Although the menu offers standard diner fare, a popular choice with the late night bunch is the Anchor Double Cheeseburger, the perfect thing after a night out on the town. Breakfast can be had 24 hours a day, but this is goetta country, so order a slab of the sausage-like concoction

of ground meat, steel-cut oats and spices with your scrambled eggs or pancakes for a real taste of the region. Or if breakfast is not your thing, go with the GLT, a goetta, lettuce and tomato sandwich; it'll be the perfect way to cap off your experience at the wonderfully seedy Anchor Grill. It's northern Kentucky's favorite place to come for kitsch and coffee any hour of the day, and that's what makes it one of the 111 Fabulous Food Finds in the state.

The Athenaeum

649 South Tenth Street
Williamsburg, Kentucky 40769
(606) 539-4105

N ot far from the Kentucky-Tennessee state line is the University of the Cumberlands, a Southern-Baptist affiliated school with roots going back to the 1880s. Part of the university is the Cumberland Inn, a state-of-the-art conference center and 50-room hotel that provides students with work opportunities to fund their education. In the Cumberland Inn you'll find the Athenaeum, an upscale dining room that opened in 1994 to offer traditional southern and eclectic fare against the scenic backdrop of the Appalachians.

True to form – an anthenaeum is an institution for the promotion of learning – rows of picture-perfect leather-bound books line the walls of the sunny dining room, where a fireplace adds a bit of cozy warmth to the club atmosphere. Oftentimes, piano music drifts between the tables, lulling guests into a pleasant stupor as they sit back and enjoy friendly service and good food.

Known for its weekday $8.99 lunch buffet that

includes salad, hot bar, beverage and dessert, the Athenaeum is a popular destination for daily continental breakfasts as well. Evening and mid-day menus include old-fashioned entrée items such as liver and onions and buttermilk-marinated catfish fried in seasoned cornmeal and served with cole slaw, hushpuppies and steak or sweet potato fries, but you'll also find a seemingly out-of-place stir fry and a pasta dish or two. There's also a Cumberland club, a triple-decker sandwich with turkey, ham, bacon, lettuce, tomato and mayo, but whatever you get, make sure you start with the signature fried green tomato salad. Fresh mixed greens with crumbled bleu cheese and crispy bacon topped with crispy green tomatoes slices are sure to become a favorite.

If the academic surroundings have inspired your curiosity, take a couple steps out of the Athenaeum and you'll be at the Cumberland Inn Museum. Among the interesting displays are stamp, coin, arrowhead, and nutcracker collections, along with the fascinating Carl Williams Cross Collection. Expand your horizons at the museum and enjoy a meal afterwards and you'll see why the Anthenaeum is one of Kentucky's Fabulous Food Finds.

19

Beaumont Inn

638 Beaumont Inn Drive
Harrodsburg, Kentucky 40330
(859) 734-3381

If you're not convinced that Kentucky is part of the South — at least culinarily speaking — take a trip to Harrodsburg's famous Beaumont Inn. Stately white columns adorn the antebellum structure, which housed a girls' school in the 19th century, and costly antiques fill the parlors and sitting rooms. There are even portraits of Confederate generals hanging on walls in the entryway. Items such as country ham, yellow-legged fried chicken, corn pudding and Robert E. Lee orange cake, a house specialty, are on the menu, and overnight guests can order biscuits and gravy, grits and cooked-to-order, corn meal batter cakes with brown sugar syrup for breakfast. The famous Duncan Hines said it was his very favorite place to eat and it receives regular accolades from such national publications as *Southern Living* magazine, so it's little wonder that the Beaumont Inn ranks high on the list of must-eat places in the Bluegrass.

Considered the state's oldest family-operated country inn by most, the Beaumont Inn has a lineage of hospitality that goes back almost a hundred years, to around 1919 when the Dedmans began inviting guests to enjoy their grand ambiance and south-

ern flair. Since generations of the Dedman family have pursued noble Kentucky pastimes such as curing hams and distilling whiskey in the Harrodsburg area, it's only fitting that Chuck and Helen Dedman and their son, Dixon, have carried this long tradition of Beaumont Inn hospitality into the 21st century. The spacious, park-like grounds of the Beaumont Inn are perfect for a leisurely stroll after their famous Sunday brunch or before turning in for the night in one the 33 guest rooms appointed with antique and period furnishings.

Although the food in the main dining room is worth the trip alone, their Old Owl Tavern offers casual dining, and a spa was recently added that allows visitors to pamper themselves even more. For a taste of the Old South, visit the Beaumont Inn and see why it's one of the state's most Fabulous Food Finds.

Beehive Tavern

101 Riverside Drive
Augusta, Kentucky 41002
(606) 756-2202

Even before you enter Augusta's Beehive Tavern, you know a unique experience is in store. Housed in an ancient brick building overlooking the Ohio River, its wisteria-covered gallery has a weathered grace that hints at bygone simplicity, a gentler and slower time when flatboats and steam wheelers plied the shadowy waters. Maybe it was this gentility that attracted Luciano Moral to the building in the 1980s. A lover of old buildings, the Cuban immigrant spent the next five years fixing up the former apothecary shop and filling it with period pieces, transforming the 1796 structure into the inviting and artistic riverside inn it is today.

At the Beehive, it's not just culinary talent that welcomes visitors, and the arias of Moral, a classically trained opera singer, can often be heard

Sauerkraut balls, a northern Kentucky specialty, are a popular appetizer at Luciano Moral's charming restaurant.

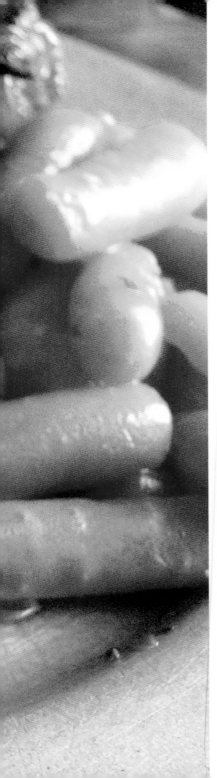

throughout the restaurant. An ardent supporter of the arts, he has played a large role in making the little river town of Augusta a special destination and his spaces are used to exhibit local prints, pastels and water colors. Nonetheless, the food is as big a draw here as the inviting interior.

Granted, you'll be won over by the painted floors, distressed tables and rustic Windsor chairs, but a taste from the modest assortment of menu items will convince you that the Beehive Tavern is one of Kentucky's Fabulous Food Finds. Although the menu changes every six weeks, appetizers will include options such as liver paté, stuffed peppers and fried sauerkraut balls, a northern Kentucky specialty that is much better than the uninitiated might expect. Among the entrées are items like pan-seared duck breast, strip steak, old-fashioned pork roast or baked chicken with apples and bleu cheese; dessert selections often include sweet specialties such as blueberry trifle and flan, the quintessential Hispanic custard.

The charming town of Augusta makes for a wonderful day trip in northern Kentucky, and the Beehive Tavern is just one attraction. The main street has a number of charming shops and restaurants and the Rosemary Clooney House — the proprietors are Steve Henry and his beauty queen wife and Augusta native, Heather Renee French, by the way — is just a block away.

Biancke's Restaurant

102 South Main Street
Cynthiana, Kentucky 41031
(859) 234-3443

If your restaurant has been around for more than 100 years, chances are someone has been doing something right. Bianke's is not only a local institution in Cynthiana, it is also a legend throughout the state, as it claims to be Kentucky's oldest, continually operated eatery. Housed in an unassuming storefront in downtown Cynthiana, Biancke's (by the way, that's pronounced 'bang-keys') came about as the brainchild of Italian immigrant Guido Biancke, who started selling fruits and vegetables soon after his arrival in 1890. Four years later, the business that would bear the family name was founded and the rest is, as they say, history. Today, recent high school graduate Mary Todd Seaman is keeping the Cynthiana tradition of hospitality and good food alive with Italian-American favorites such as baked spaghetti and down-home Bluegrass fare like hot browns and fried green tomatoes. At Biancke's the tomatoes are a favorite and they're sliced thin and served with a tangy, creamy sauce flavored with tomato and horseradish. The "Big Joe," a burger topped with melted cheese, special sauce and dill pickles is another signature item, but regulars also rave about the homemade cream pies, which occupy a place of honor in a display case at the front of the restaurant.

Although the place has been spruced up over the years, the interior of Biancke's still sports visible reminders from the past today. An old hand-painted sign in faded hues of pink and green, a wall-mounted crank phone from the turn of the last century, walls filled with framed high school class pictures from the early 1900s — these are just some of the mementos of previous generations that patronized Biancke's for its potato soup, pork tenderloin sandwiches and fried catfish. The polished green tile floors still gleam like they used to and out-of-towners and locals alike flock in for good food and good company any time of the day — this makes Biancke's one of many Fabulous Food Finds in the Bluegrass.

Big Bubba Buck's Belly Bustin' BBQ Bliss

1802 Main Street
Munfordville, Kentucky 42765
(270) 524-3333

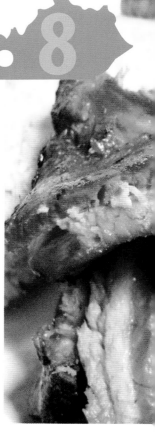

8

Big Bubba Buck's Belly Bustin' BBQ Bliss – now that's a mouthful. Call it BBBBBBB, for short. Robert Chapman, aka Buck, says he and his wife needed to make some extra money, so they started selling their barbecue at a local festival – soon Big Bubba Buck's Belly Bustin' BBQ Bliss was born. Today it's a popular stop for travelers passing by on I-65, and it's not uncommon to find half a dozen semis in the gravel parking lot next to the little blue shack the locals refer to simply as "Buck's." In fact, according to Chapman, 90 percent of the customers are truck drivers.

Walk into the tiny interior with the patriotic décor and a handful of tables, and someone at the counter will ask you if it's "eat in or carry out?" Ask them what to get, and they'll

tell you "barbecue." Since barbecue is the specialty of the house, ribs and pulled pork are two hot items. Buck smokes the pork shoulder himself for 30-some hours, so by the time it arrives on your plate, it is meltingly good and has a nice amount of smoke flavor that pairs well with the homemade sauce, which is a bit sweet and not too hot.

In addition to fried pork chops, there are also items like catfish, barbecue tacos, fried bologna, slaw dogs, and taco salad for main courses. Now and then, Buck will even offer hickory-smoked hamburgers as the daily special, served with two sides, dessert and drink. Sides include "taters" in many forms — salad, fried, and sweet potato fries dusted with cinnamon and sugar — and pinto beans, fried "maters," collards, fried corn, barbecue beans, and fried okra. Popular desserts include the blueberry cobbler and homemade 'nana puddin'. Because the 'cue is down-home good and because I love alliteration, Big Bubba Buck's is one of our Fabulous Food Finds indeed.

BIG MOMMA'S SOUL FOOD

4532 West Broadway
Louisville, Kentucky 40211
(502) 772-9580

ting at home," she adopted the name.

Today Big Momma's is synonymous with big portions of no-frills fare and it's not uncommon to find the tiny eatery crowded with customers studying the day's selection of food that is invitingly displayed in large trays behind a Plexiglas wall. The choices vary and some days patrons will find things like fried chicken, pork chops smothered in gravy, ox tails, buttery mashed potatoes, braised cabbage and green beans mixed with great chunks of ham; on others there'll be salmon croquettes, baked chicken, meatloaf, macaroni and cheese, okra and lima beans. Sweet, cakelike cornbread is available every day, and on Sundays greens are always on the menu, although they usually sell out in a couple of hours. "Cooking greens is a lot of work," says Big Momma, "and we usually go through five bushels of them." Because it's the best place for soul food and slow-cooked collards around, Big Momma's is one of Louisville's many Fabulous Food Finds.

"I put soul in it and that's why I call it soul food," says Big Momma, the proprietor of the namesake restaurant where she serves up hearty batches of down-home southern cooking in Louisville's West End. Though she is not very big at all, Big Momma, whose real name is Jesse Davis, explains that children in the neighborhood stuck her with the moniker back when she "was kinda heavy." In 2004, in need of a name for the restaurant she opened across the street from Shawnee Park after being "tired of sit-

There's only a couple seats here, so most customers order items such as smothered pork chops or fried chicken to go at this basic eatery. Luxury's not on the menu, just good food.

Billy Ray's

101 North Front Avenue
Prestonsburg, Kentucky 41653
(606) 886-1744

Situated at the base of a hill where the old Prestonsburg toll bridge used to stand, Billy Ray's is a wonderful place for breakfast seven days a week, as any regular will tell you. Often packed with locals from surrounding Appalachian towns who freely circulate while exchanging greetings and gossip, the place is known for its homemade biscuits and hearty

34

meals designed to put a little meat on your bones. Popular morning combos include two eggs with fried potatoes and a choice of meat such as pork tenderloin or country sausage — and the "hungry man," a plate with three eggs, biscuits and gravy, delicious home fries that are more like thick-cut potato chips, and a choice of several different meats, the country ham being very popular.

The décor at Billy Ray's is understated, and owners Sheila and Lee Collins have used memorabilia from local and college sports teams to add a comfortable touch to the walls. Lunchtime is usually busy as well, with many of the stools at the long counter running the length of the dining room occupied by patrons in search of the "pool room" burger, a creation that hearkens back to the building's former days as a billiards hall. It's at the counter where guests with a sweet tooth will find what they've been looking for: an enticing series of glass-domed dessert stands and plates with a variety of homemade pies, cakes and pastries. Although locals swear by the carrot cake and cherry pie, Billy Ray's is known for its apple dumplings. Served on a hot plate with vanilla ice cream and cinnamon glaze, it's the perfect end to a nice dinner or lunch, but it's just as good all by itself with a cup of coffee on a lazy weekend afternoon. Good breakfasts and hearty mountain fare make Billy Ray's one of eastern Kentucky's Fabulous Food Finds.

Bistro Le Relais
at Bowman Field

2817 Taylorsville Road
Louisville, Kentucky 40205
(502) 451-9020

The food at Louisville's Bistro Le Relais may be French, but the setting is pure Americana. Situated at historic Bowman Field — established in 1919, it is the longest continuously operating, general aviation airport in the United States — Le Relais offers a grand dining experience like no other in the Bluegrass. Housed in the vintage art deco Administration Building from the 1920s, the restaurant has a front row seat on the tarmac, and with a little imagination, it's easy to see it exactly as Charles Lindbergh did when he landed the famous *Spirit of St. Louis* on the runway in 1927.

At today's Le Relais, deco-inspired style from the 1940s with plush banquettes, burled-wood walls,

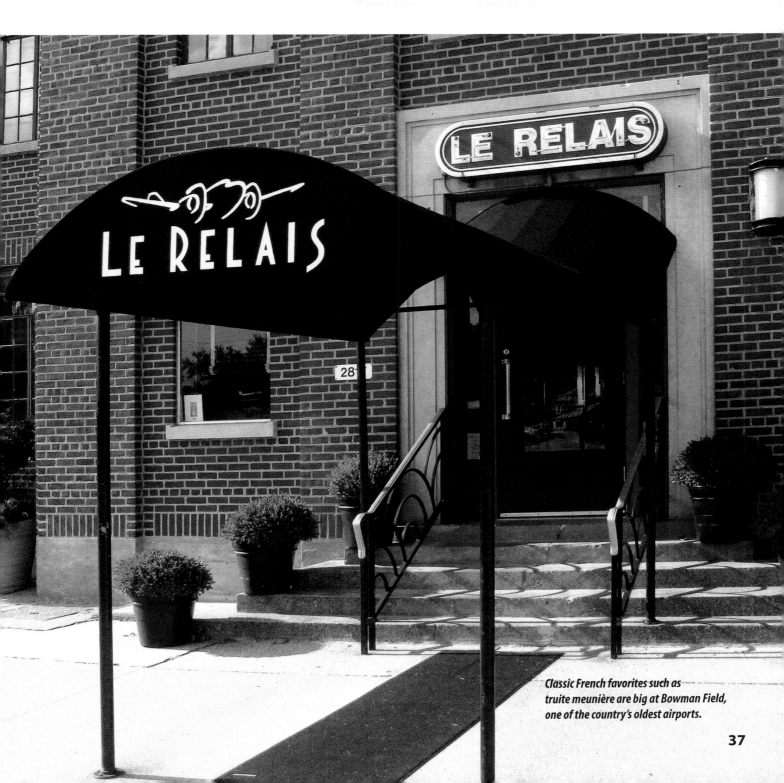

Classic French favorites such as truite meunière are big at Bowman Field, one of the country's oldest airports.

and cozy white-clothed tables recaptures an ambiance that makes the perfect backdrop for exquisite French cuisine. On the menu, owner Anthony Dike offers his guests a variety of seasonal dishes showcasing the finest, freshest ingredients and brought to the table by a relaxed staff of first-class servers. Although the menu changes frequently, French bistro classics such as escargots, mussels steamed in white wine, steak frites, crêpes and pâtés can usually be found in the lineup. Other standards include the truite meunière — fillets of trout sautéed in browned butter with lemon and parsley — and luscious sweet favorites like mousse au chocolade and crème brûlée. Dessert is especially nice on the outdoor deck — it's usually a less formal crowd, and when the sun goes down, it provides wonderfully romantic views of the airport — and live jazz is on the menu Sunday evenings. Classic French flair and a historic location — that's why Bistro Le Relais is one of the state's most Fabulous Food Finds.

Boone Tavern

100 Main Street
Berea, Kentucky 40404
(859) 985-3700

steeped in rich Appalachian traditions and synonymous with arts, crafts, and music, the town of Berea is also known for its tuition-free college founded by ardent abolitionists and radical reformers in 1855. Today the quiet campus provides a bucolic setting for a number of majestic buildings, one of them being the historic Boone Tavern, which celebrated 100 years of hospitality in 2009.

For generations of Kentuckians, the Boone Tavern has come to symbolize the gentility and refined home cooking that epitomized the hotel experience of mid-1900s America. During that time the restaurant earned no small degree of national fame under the management of Richard T. Hougen, whose culinary

legacy includes such dishes as pork chops the tricky way, chicken flakes in a bird's nest, Kentucky chess pie, and yeasty dinner rolls. The spoon bread — a creamy corn bread soufflé served before every meal — has earned a name for itself as well, contributing to a rich tradition of southern-inspired foods that is kept alive by chef Jeffrey Newman today.

This tradition also includes a sense of hospitality cultivated by the friendly student workers and dedicated staff that toil away in a cavernous kitchen straight from the 1940s. Bruce Alcorn and Rawleigh Johnson have worked in the kitchen for more than 30 years and remember the days before the nearby Interstate was put in, the days when the Boone Tavern was on the main thoroughfare and they served 200 to 300 people a day. Although the crowds have dwindled somewhat, visit the Boone Tavern and you'll see why Duncan Hines consistently included it in his recommendations for the best places to eat. If it's good enough for Duncan Hines, then it's good enough for me — and that's what makes it one of Kentucky's Fabulous Food Finds.

The dining room at the Boone Tavern was a favorite of Kentucky son Duncan Hines.

Bourbons Bistro

2255 Frankfort Avenue
Louisville, Kentucky 40206
(502) 894-8838

Life in the Bluegrass, the state that produces most of the whiskey made in the U.S., has a reputation for being unhurried and pleasantly slow, laid back and mellow, just like good bourbon. It's only fitting, then, that establishments devoted primarily to the joys of America's national spirit have been taking root in our limestone-rich soil. One of them is Bourbons Bistro in Louisville, a casually elegant eatery which opened in 2005.

Housed in an older brick structure on Frankfort Avenue's restaurant row, Bourbons Bistro combines comfortable, cozy surroundings and innovative Kentucky-themed cuisine to produce an all-round enjoyable dining experience. All things considered, the wine list is more than substantial, but bourbon is the obvious libation of choice here. The list that proprietors Jason Brauner and John Morrison, along with chef David Crouch, have designed has to be the most extensive in the area, with a total of more than 130 different sorts. Prices start at $5 for many labels and go all the way to $45 for a shot of the choicest Kentucky dew.

BOURBONS
BISTRO
EST. 05

Bourbons Bistro is a popular stop on Louisville's Urban Bourbon Trail.

*(above)The bourbon brown — David Crouch's twist on the local favorite includes roast pork shoulder and a fried egg.
(right)Braised bison short ribs.*

The chef has fortunately devised a thoughtful menu with selections that can just as easily be enjoyed with a slosh of Evan Williams on the rocks or a Woodford Reserve Manhattan as they can with a glass of sauvignon blanc or merlot. The bill of fare begins with starters that might include fried green tomatoes or diver scallops with pickled green beans, and salads such as a lettuce wedge with bleu cheese, red onion and tomato or Kentucky Bibb lettuce with ginger-mint dressing, strawberries and pecans.

Entrées such as hand-pattied burgers with Kentucky Cheddar and iron-seared filet of beef with Yukon gold mashed potatoes and bourbon demi-glaze round out the dinner menu, which changes frequently. Dessert selections reflect seasonal preferences as well and include house favorites such as chocolate bourbon bread pudding and strawberry rhubarb crisp, served hot from the oven in miniature cast-iron skillets. Bourbon's on the menu at this Crescent Hill bistro and that's why it counts as one of many Fabulous Food Finds in Kentucky.

Bread of Life Café

5369 South US 127
Liberty, Kentucky 42539
(606) 787-6110

14.

The Galilean Children's Home is a non-profit organization that cares for children from all over the world, many of whom have been abused, neglected, or are in need of medical treatment. Michigan transplants Jerry and Sandy Tucker began the Casey County institution in 1986, providing care for some 800 children over the years, in addition to adopting 25 children on their own while building a community where they could grow up safely and happily. Since the Mennonite couple relied heavily on donations from the public and fundraisers for support, it seemed only natural that they would one day start a home-cooking restaurant, not just as a means to raise extra money, but also as a way to provide those in their charge valuable real-life and work experience. So by eating here, you're helping in more ways than one.

At the Bread of Life Café, the staff is very friendly, and the interior is immaculate. You can have the $8.99 buffet, which includes drink, desert and a salad bar with a good variety of vegetables and dressings, or you can order items à la carte. Although you'll find some out-of-place options such as a grilled southwestern chicken melt or steak quesadilla, most of the

offerings on the menu focus on old-fashioned standards and down-home favorites, with home-grown produce and homemade bread featured heavily.

One place where the bread is put to good use is in the sandwiches at Bread of Life Café. In addition to a four-ounce rib-eye with lettuce and tomato, hot sandwiches include grilled pork tenderloin, a corned beef reuben, southern fried catfish, and the popular turkey Manhattan, which has gravy-smothered mashed potatoes and turkey strips mounded atop a thick slice of fluffy white bread. There's also a sandwich featuring the local favorite,

Penn's country ham, which has been produced in the area since 1957.

A center cut of Penn's country ham, served up with a choice of fixings such as baked potato, onion rings or sweet potato fries, is also available in the entrée section, where there's a variety of pork, chicken, beef and seafood items. And if you're interested in taking some home with you, you can pick up Penn's country ham at the adjacent shop that sells fresh baked goods, sweets and Amish products as well. The food is good, and so is the cause, and that makes the Bread of Life Café a Fabulous Food Find for me.

Broadbent's Deli

257 Mary Blue Road
Kuttawa, Ketucky 42055
(270) 388-0609

In the Bluegrass, country ham seems to pop up whenever there's a special occasion. But in Kuttawa you don't have to wait for Christmas or Easter to enjoy the local favorite, because Broadbent's Deli offers a yummy lineup of sandwiches and breakfast items featuring the star product all year long. The "city ham" sandwich features layers of hickory-smoked pork with mustard, sweet pickles and Colby and Cheddar cheeses on sour dough bread, and the "sweet & sassy" has slices of boiled country ham dressed with Broadbent's tangy mustard, sliced apple and smoked Cheddar on Sister Shubert rolls. The pepper bacon BLT is popular with the locals, and a favorite of Broadbent owners Beth and Ronny Drennan is the BBQ ham with smoked ham, spicy mayo, Cheddar and sweet dill pickles. There's even an "uptown" bologna sandwich with spicy mayo and a breakfast bite with sausage and cheese.

Western Kentucky is known for producing award-winning country hams — think Newsom's, Meacham's and Harper's — however Broadbent's holds the unique distinction of its yearly Grand Champion Ham at the Kentucky State Fair. In 2010, it sold for a record $99,688.47 per pound, raising a total of $1.6 million for various charities, so you know it's going to be good. If you've got a little time, wave down Beth or Ronny Drennan and they'll tell you a little more about their famous hams. Or have them take you back

for a quick tour of the facility and you'll see how they smoke their hams and sausages today, carrying on the century-old Broadbent tradition since purchasing the business in 1999.

On site is a small gift shop where you can browse the assortment of Broadbent products, in addition to a collection of Kentucky cookbooks, and a huge selection of jams, sauces, condiments, candies, teas, and more. Before you go, you can also stock up on a supply of deli meats and Kenny's Farmhouse cheeses at the front counter. And don't forget the whole ham – it wouldn't be a special occasion without it! That's what makes Broadbent Deli one of our Fabulous Food Finds.

Buddy's Pizza

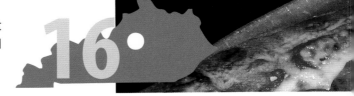

Buddy's is Frankfort's only brick-oven pizzeria and the owner is Mike Hedden, a Kentucky native who has been cooking for more than 20 years. The restaurant is named after Buddy, a special dog from Hedden's college days at the University of Kentucky, and, hardly surprising, it is especially popular among dog lovers. In fact, Buddy's has gained such a reputation with pet owners that many pop in with pictures of their four-legged friends and display them on the K-9 Wall of Fame. Since opening in 2006, it's become a sort of ritual for people to stop by with a framed picture of their dogs and drink a toast in Fido's honor. They usually have a pizza as well.

The "Meathead" is one their most popular pies. The New York-style, thin-crust creation has a base of molten cheese topped with discs of sliced Italian sausage and pepperoni, slabs of Canadian bacon, crumbled bacon and crumbled Italian sausage. The crust, though pliable, has crisp edges and just enough charring to make it the perfect match to the toppings. The pizza is good, and the prices are affordable as well: a large, meat-laden pizza and a beer cost just $20.00. Every day except Sunday, Buddy's opens for lunch and stays open till at least 9:00 p.m. Single slices go for $2.50 plus tax, and a popular lunch deal is a huge slice of pizza with a tossed salad and a bottomless soft drink for just $6.00. Great brick-oven pizza and a place to hang a picture of your favorite pet — this combination makes Buddy's Pizza one of Frankfort's Fabulous Food Finds.

Burger Boy

1625 South Main Street
London, Kentucky 40741
(606) 864-2675

When Dean Ramsey Sr. opened his London restaurant in October 1961 he probably didn't know it would become one of Laurel County's most beloved culinary landmarks — nor did he ever think the establishment would be going strong a half century later. Today, however, the Burger Boy is a popular destination for legions of loyal customers and curious first-timers, many of them passing by on nearby I-75; since it's open 24 hours a day, there's usually an interesting crowd to boot.

Even though Ramsey's son Robbie took over in 1982, little has changed at the Burger Boy over the years — including the hallmark red and yellow sign with the bumpkin burger boy outside in the parking lot. Today visitors find the same booth-and-table layout skirting a sit-down counter where guests can still watch the short-order cook prepare meals while catching up on the news of the day. Like the rest of the place, the menu at Robbie Ramsey's eatery has seen no dramatic changes and the focus is still on traditional American breakfast served all day long. But be forewarned: they usually start running short on the homemade biscuits around noon — and the daily special, the hot roast beef sandwich with mashed potatoes and gravy for only $5.99, is only available from 11:00 a.m. to 9:00 p.m.

Aside from a goodly selection of

sandwiches and several soups and salads, the rest of the menu consists primarily of entrée items divided into pork, seafood, steak and chicken categories. The "Bauter better chicken," hand-breaded and fried fresh daily has earned a faithful following by devotees who consider it the very best in the state. Crispy and delicious, it is best followed by a piece of strawberry pie when it's in season. Because there's "nothin' fancy, just good food" you'll agree that London's Burger Boy is one the state's Fabulous Food Finds indeed.

Burger Shakes

219 East New Circle Road
Lexington, Kentucky 40505
(859) 299-4113

It's not often that you find an old-fashioned stand where your burgers are wrapped in waxed paper and carried away in a plain brown paper bag, but that's how it is at the low brick building with the red roof on Lexington's New Circle Road. The menu is simple as well, with basics such as hamburgers, cheeseburgers, fries and milkshakes gaining a faithful clientele ever since I & I Inc. opened in 1957. Most locals, however, don't know it as I & I Inc. and refer to it simply as "Burger Shakes" instead. Look at the sign on top of the building and you'll see their inspiration: Burgers. Shakes. 84 cents. It's a no-nonsense declaration of the two staples on the menu, both of which go for — you guessed it — 84 cents.

If you're asking what the I & I Inc. stands for, the I is for the last name of the brothers from Cumberland — Samuel Isaacs and Joe Isaac — who started selling burgers for 19 cents, fries for 14 cents and cokes for a dime in Lexington in the 1950s. The discrepancy in the spelling of the last names arose after a clerical error in the army resulted in an s being added to Samuel's last name, but do the math and you'll see there's been only a modest increase in prices over the years, something that has kept crowds coming.

But the cheap prices wouldn't be enough if the food wasn't good. They only start cooking your burger after you've placed the order, and the thin and crispy fries always come out piping hot, because they toss them into the fryer after you place your order as well. The same is true of the fish and chicken sandwiches, items that were added to the line up in the 1990s when Samuel and Joe turned the business over to their daughters and their husbands. Other than a few new menu items, not much has changed since Sharyn and Joe Clements and Sammy Lou and Tom Lilly took over — in fact they still use the old change machine that uses 50 cent coins that have to be preordered from Cincinnati — and it's likely to remain one of the few places where you can get a hamburger, fries and a frosty shake for under $3.00 for a number of years to come. Burgers cooked to order for only 84 cents are what make this one of our Fabulous Food Finds.

Burke's Bakery

121 West Main Street
Danville, Kentucky 40422
(859) 236-5661

Settled in 1783, Danville easily lays claim to being one of the most historic cities in the state. Not only is it home to prestigious Centre College, this town of some 16,000 residents also enjoys a reputation as the birthplace of Bluegrass and as a city of historic firsts, including the first courthouse in Kentucky. In addition, Kentucky's first constitution was written here in 1792 and Constitution Square forms the heart of Danville today. Across from Constitution square, on Main Street, is Burke's Bakery, another of the city's historical treasures and the place where locals have come to stock up on glazed donuts, birthday cakes and other homemade goodies for generations. Give them a try and you'll see why people keep coming back for more.

In addition to macaroons and fondant drops, Burke's has old-fashioned favorites like iced chunks of angel food cake.

But don't ask how long they've been coming back for more, because no one at Burke's seems to know. "I don't know the exact year the bakery started up, but we've been at the current location for at least 50 years," says Patty Burke, the town temptress of tasty treats, who is often behind the counter pushing delights such as cream horns, butterflake rolls and chocolate macaroons. "But the bakery was going strong long before then." One thing Burke does know is that her father-in-law, Sam Burke, started working for his father in the current location in April 1946, and with her husband, Joe, and their son, Jody, five generations of Burkes have kept the bakery going.

Voted the best in the state by readers of *Kentucky Monthly* magazine, Burke's has also been written up in other publications, including *Southern Living* magazine, which has touted the famous salt-rising bread and doughnut holes, something Patty says are hard to keep in stock. But that's not all you'll find at Burke's: in addition to home-baked pies, cakes, breads and rolls, the shelves are home to gingerbread men, an old-fashioned favorite that most bakeries only offer at Christmas time. But be forewarned: "I can't keep in them in stock," she says. "Mothers come in regularly and buy them up to mail them to their children at college." Other popular sweets are fondant drops, spice cups and glazed chunks of angel food cake, but there are also dressed eggs and deli spreads such as pimento cheese, ham salad, and chicken salad, all made on site daily. Try the baked bestsellers at Burke's Bakery and you'll see why this Danville institution is a Fabulous Food Find.

Café at the Kentucky Artisan Center

975 Walnut Meadow Road
Berea, Kentucky 40403
(859) 985-5448

Conveniently located alongside Interstate 75 at exit 77, just 40 miles south of Lexington, and only a couple of miles from downtown Berea, the "Folk Arts and Craft Capital of Kentucky," is the Kentucky Artisan Center. Aside from full rest stop services and the chance to hop on board for a free 40-minute trolley tour of downtown Berea, the 25,000 square-foot facility offers opportunities to shop for Kentucky products, explore crafts and history from across the state, browse books by local authors and even enjoy regional cuisine at an on-site cafeteria-style restaurant.

The menu includes an assortment of fresh-made sandwiches, salads and soups, however for an old-fashioned taste of Kentucky, head to the "traditional" section where you'll find an ever-changing se-

Tomato pie and hot browns – two regular lunch favorites at the Kentucky Artisan Center.

lection of down-home entrées and staples that include seasoned green beans, tomato pie, corn pudding, soup beans and bourbon bread pudding. From 11 a.m. to 2 p.m. chef Kathleen Purcell serves daily lunch specials with two sides and bread for just $6.95. For choices guests usually find meatloaf on Mondays, hot browns on Tuesdays, pan-fried chicken on Wednesdays, pork loin and corn bread dressing on Thursdays, fried catfish with hushpuppies on Fridays – and on Saturdays and Sundays there's barbecue and carved roast beef. To finish everything off, there are cakes, cobblers and cookies, as well as John Conti coffee and Valentine's gourmet ice cream.

The Kentucky Artisan Center at Berea is open to the public daily, from 8 in the morning till 8 at night, with café service from 8:30 a.m. to 5 p.m. Because you can fill up on great Kentucky fare and then shop for the best hand-made products in the state seven days a week, the Café at the Kentucky Artisan Center is one of the best Fabulous Food Find around.

Cantuckee Diner

12 Carol Road
Winchester, Kentucky 40391
(859) 744-7377

In Winchester they spell it the old-fashioned way: Cantuckee. Maybe it's because old-fashioned describes the style of cooking served by Hallie Moore and Dollie Zehnder, the two sisters from Breathitt County who opened this rustic diner right off of I-64 in 1988. Look for the large sign with the horse's head and horseshoes and it'll be easy

enough to find. The exterior is covered in rough-hewn planking and the interior sports lots of knotty pine and hard wooden booths — and chances are it's usually bustling with activity for two reasons. First, they open early and stay open late. Second, the prices can hardly be beat. It's very easy for two people to go in and eat their fill for $10 apiece. Aside from breakfast fare, the menu at Cantuckee Diner has lots of regional favorites such as fried chicken, roast beef and mashed potatoes, country ham, and chicken livers and daily specials often feature popular standards like meatloaf and chicken and dumplings.

Without a doubt, the best way to enjoy the variety at Cantuckee Diner is the $9.99 all-you-can-eat buffet and salad bar. Friday and Saturday nights, a steam table is laden with hot pans of fried frog legs, barbecued ribs, pork chops and the sisters' wonderful fried catfish; the cornmeal breading is oh-so-light and perfectly crispy without a hint of excess grease. Savory sides such as the macaroni and cheese, green beans, spiced turnip and mustard greens, broccoli and cheese casserole, and soup beans are worth the $9.99 alone and it's not uncommon to find vegetarians helping themselves to a meal at the buffet. Included in the buffet are a basket of hot yeast rolls and corn bread and a choice of dessert afterwards. The coconut cream pie, rich and not too sweet with a dusting of shredded coconut, is just as good as grandma would have made and makes the perfect sweet ending to dinner or lunch at Cantuckee Diner. Because they've got one of the best buffets around, you'll agree that Cantuckee Diner is one of our most Fabulous Food Finds in Kentucky.

Catfish Kitchen

136 Teal Run Circle
Benton, Kentucky 42025
(270) 362-7306

When you're in the scenic Land between the Lakes in western Kentucky and catfish is on your mind, there's one place you have to go: the Catfish Kitchen. Wes Davis owns the popular restaurant near Draffenville, and for nearly 30 years its setting has been as big a draw as the food. Nestled alongside a small lake where the fish are raised and caught, the Catfish Kitchen is housed in a low stone-and-timber structure chock full of eye candy that includes taxidermy, outdoor paraphernalia and random antiques hanging from the rafters. In addition, there are large picture windows that afford pleasant views of the pond, where visitors are often found feeding the fish before or after their meals.

As soon as you sit down, delicious hushpuppies, creamy slaw and beans with ham are set down at your table in the Catfish Kitchen.

Although you'll find other items on the menu — jumbo shrimp, clams, baked fish, and Cajun chicken breast, for example — fried catfish is king here. The "full" order comes with three tender filets lightly fried in seasoned cornmeal and served with home fries, French fries or baked potato, in addition to a hearty garnish of sliced onion, lemon wedge and green onion. But as tasty as the fish is, the best part of a visit to the Catfish Kitchen is the extras that magically appear on your table as soon as you take your seat. Whatever the entrées, the table will also get a dish of creamy cole slaw, a steaming bowl of savory beans with big chunks of ham, and a heap of slightly sweet, perfectly crispy hushpuppies. The combination is such a winner that many people make a meal out of it and opt for the all-you-can-eat "bowl of beans" with cole slaw and hushpuppies. Tasty catfish, delicious beans and ham, and the best hushpuppies in western Kentucky — these are what make the Catfish Kitchen one of western Kentucky's Fabulous Food Finds.

Charlie's Steakhouse

14850 US 41A South
Oak Grove, Kentucky 42262
(270) 439-4592

23

I t is a big night-on-the-town kind of place where cocktails and steak signify the high life," says seasoned food writer and road food expert Michael Stern of Charlie's Steakhouse, a western Kentucky classic known for its plush upholstered booths, large-scale luxury ambience and tender full-flavored meat. It's hardly surprising, then, that visitors have been known to drive over a hundred miles just to sink their teeth into generous chops and steaks like the signature Charlie's Special, a strapping porterhouse rubbed with garlic and spice that is broiled to perfection and served with a huge baked potato on the side. The out-of-town visitors notwithstanding, Charlie's is hugely popular with the locals, many of them servicemen and their families from nearby Fort Campbell who have patronized the restaurant since it opened in 1949.

73

Much like the décor, which is vintage 1950s and 60s, the menu has hardly changed over the years at Charlie's. In addition to appetizers such as fresh shrimp cocktails and relish bowls with olives and celery, there are old-fashioned salads like ham, bacon and egg chef salads and sliced pineapples with peaches and pears to start your meal. And although there is a good selection of non-beef items — you can order smoked pork chops, frog legs, fried oysters, chicken breasts, broiled salmon and lobster tails — most come to Charlie's for the steaks. Aside from the legendary porterhouse, filets and kabobs star in the lineup, and there's a popular sirloin for two when guests come in search of a romantic dinner.

It's not hard to find Charlie's Steakhouse — just follow your nose and look for the huge steer on the stone-clad building. Whether you drive one mile or one hundred, classic steaks and vintage supper club feel make dinner at Charlie's Steakhouse worth the trip — not to mention one of the Fabulous Food Finds in western Kentucky.

Claudia Sanders Dinner House

3202 Shelbyville Road
Shelbyville, Kentucky 40065
(502) 633-5600

In 1959, Claudia Sanders accompanied her soon-to-be-famous husband, the Colonel, from Corbin, Kentucky to Shelbyville, where they took up residence in a one-hundred-twenty-five-year-old dwelling known as Blackwood Hall. The stately home would also serve as the base of operations for Kentucky Fried Chicken, and booming business eventually resulted in the construction of an adjacent building that later became the famed dinner house where Claudia Sanders would showcase her own brand of southern cooking. Although she and the Colonel have long since vacated the premises, their spirit of hospitality still lives on at the renowned eatery and Claudia's down-home style of southern cooking has become something of a regional culinary icon.

It almost came to an end in May 1999, however, when a fire broke out and destroyed the original dinner house. Fortunately, Tommy and Cherry Settle rebuilt, doing their best to keep alive the gracious hospitality and generous portions Claudia Sanders made the hallmark of her restaurant. The present structure was enlarged to 24,000 square feet and can sit up to 700 guests at a time, many of whom arrive by the busload. A porcelain-tiled foyer with a grand antebellum-styled staircase greets guest as they arrive, and to the right is the gift shop and the receptionist who will guide them to one of four elegantly decorated dining rooms.

Hardly a surprise, fried chicken enjoys a place of prominence on the menu at Claudia Sanders, but there are plenty of options for those looking for something different. Popular dinner selections include fried sugar-cured country ham with red-eye gravy, grilled center-cut pork chops, and baked Kentucky trout. Claudia's hot brown sandwich and the eight vegetable platter with baked apples, Harvard beets, green beans, mock oysters, corn pudding, breaded stewed tomatoes, creamed spinach and mashed potatoes are favorites as well. Those with a sweet tooth enjoy homemade desserts such as Mom Blakeman's chess pie, fruit cobblers and Claudia's chocolate pecan pie. Most of these favorites are available on the popular buffet, but whether you line up with the hungry tourists or sit down and order from the menu, you're bound to see why Claudia Sanders is a Fabulous Food Find.

Coach Lamp Restaurant & Pub

751 Vine Street
Louisville, Kentucky 40204
(502) 583-9165

25

Despite the devastation wrought by Hurricane Katrina in Louisiana, some good did come of the situation when cities like Louisville received an influx of creative transplants from the Big Easy. One of them was Richard Lowe, a New Orleans chef who now cooks at the Coach Lamp Restaurant & Pub in the Original Highlands area of Louisville. Housed in a structure from 1872 that reportedly served as a stage coach stop, the location also had a pub run by Dominick Maier. A signature item at Maier's Bar and Grill was the roast beef and mashed potato plate, and the Coach Lamp still

Lowe's Cajun version of the hot brown has pan-roasted oysters with bacon and rosemary-infused cream sauce.

Cornmeal fried artichokes with buttermilk dip are a popular way to start the meal at the Coach Lamp.

offers it on its lunch menu today, along with traditional daily specials in the blue plate vein such as fried chicken or meat loaf with sides such as green beans seasoned with onions and smoky ham and creamy mashed potatoes.

Although the menu includes an eclectic mix of southern comfort food and dinner classics such as breaded pork cutlets smothered in sausage gravy, Lowe shows a preference for Cajun and Creole dishes that pay homage to his Louisiana roots. Next to tournedos of pork glazed with molasses and root beer, diners will find standards such as crawfish étouffée and barbecued shrimp. In addition, customers will find dishes with Kentucky connections such as the bourbon chicken, a succulent breast sandwiched between layers of flaky puff pastry and finished with a creamy caramel bourbon sauce. There's even a Cajun hot brown, a distant cousin of the Bluegrass original that has a skillet full of oysters roasted in a cream sauce with bacon and rosemary.

With the abundance of wood, whitewashed brick, and vibrant contemporary paintings by Louisville artist Jay Robert Goldstein, the Coach Lamp is an inviting stop for lunch or dinner. Antique fixtures including the back bar from an old post office lend the Coach Lamp a bit of laid-back refinement that make it just as much at home in New Orleans as in the heart of Kentucky's largest city. That's why it's one of our Fabulous Food Finds.

Colonial Cottage Inn

3140 Dixie Highway
Erlanger, Kentucky 41018
(859) 341-4498

26

Owned and operated by the family of Noelle and Matt Grimes, Colonial Cottage Inn has been a northern Kentucky mainstay since 1933 when Erlanger resident Clara Rich opened to give her Depression-weary neighbors "a place that feels like home." All these years later, her goal of providing large helpings of good food at affordable prices keeps the restaurant hopping during the peak times of breakfast, lunch and dinner. The dinner menu is headlined by steak, seafood and down-home staples such as country ham and pork chops, and the pan-fried half chicken and the liver and onions with gravy are among the most popular items. In addition, the Colonial Cottage is as good a place as any to try one of the regional staples, goetta. Pronounced "getta," this sausage-like concoction of ground pork with oats and spices hearkens back to the culinary influence of German immigrants in the Cincinnati area. The cooks at the Colonial Cottage serve goetta from Glier's Meats in a variety of ways: a goetta reuben with fries, a deluxe goetta burger and a goetta wrap, just to name a few. You can even get it in an order of goetta nachos where it's browned with spices and served over tortilla chips with jalapeños and cheddar cheese sauce.

Goetta also makes an appearance for breakfast, which is served all day long; in fact, a marquis out front brags "goetta and

eggs served any time." Try the goetta hash and eggs, or the homemade biscuit with goetta, egg and cheese. If goetta's not your thing, try the Colonial Favorite, a hearty start to the day that includes two eggs to order with home fries and toast or biscuits, and a choice of country ham or two pork chops. The pork chops are lightly dredged in flour and fried till crispy, moist and delicious. The Colonial Cottage is also known for its hot slaw and daily selection of soups such as the navy bean and beef barley. It's been serving up good food since 1933, and this makes it one of the oldest Fabulous Food Finds in the state.

Corbett's:
An American Place

5050 Norton Healthcare Boulevard
Louisville, Kentucky 40241
(502) 327-5058

Photos by Dan Dry

When famed Louisville restaurateur Dean Corbett converted Louisville's historic Von Allman mansion into an upscale eatery, he pulled out all the stops in anticipation of bringing five-star elegance to the Bluegrass dining scene. "I really believe this will challenge the definition of fine dining in Louisville, and we hope to show our guests a new level of elegance with cutting-edge technology and creative cuisine," says Corbett, who assembled an all-star team of managers to join him in overseeing operations.

Meticulous planning has addressed every detail from the in-house water purification system down to the ironing board and iron in the spacious employee dressing room. To start with, Corbett hired Meg Vogt Interior Designs to create an overall look that would foster a contemporary feel, while preserving historic elements in the 100-year-old home. Custom plantation shutters allow natural light to enhance the beauty of the refurbished mahogany floors, and walls sport textured wallpaper with warm colors in shades of teal, beige, green and brown that blanket the rooms. Lighting fixtures include Boyd lighting sconces and pendulum lights, and candles in heavy Orrefors crystal holders also add to the ambiance, and specially milled damask satin band linen covers tables topped with fine Fortessa bone china and silver from Sam Bonnet. Stylish stemware comes from German glassmaker Schott Zwiesel with some specialty pieces from Rona.

Corbett's menu showcases the abundance of local purveyors as well as the best ingredients from around the world. Guests may select from an à la carte menu or choose five-course tastings for $65 and nine-course tastings for $100 for the ultimate in Kentucky fine dining. Although the menu changes based on the seasonality of ingredients, guests can expect to find items such as Sonoma veal with smoked sweet potato, chestnuts and truffled jus, or Okinawa potato ravioli with leek fondue, garlic and chives.

The Chef's Tasting Room, which accommodates eight, offers not only a specially designed tasting menu, but also the opportunity for guests to interact with Corbett and his team through state-of-the-art audio/visual equipment. Pop in for lunch or dinner at Corbett's and you'll understand why many think it's one of the state's most Fabulous Food Finds.

The interactive Chef's Table at Dean Corbett's newest restaurant makes for a fun outing with a group of friends.

Cottage Inn Restaurant

570 Eastern Parkway
Louisville, Kentucky 40217
(502) 637-4325

They call it the Cottage Inn Restaurant because that's how it started out — as a cottage along Louisville's tree-lined Eastern Parkway. In 1929 the inviting stone house became a neighborhood delicatessen operated by Harvey Board, who converted the front two rooms into double dining areas separated by open arches. This in turn eventually transformed into a sit-down restaurant that catered to employees of nearby St. Joseph's Infirmary and students at the University of Louisville. Today, the décor remains simple and unassuming, with wainscoted beige walls, sturdy wooden tables and chairs and an oversize picture window offering pleasant views of the garden outside. The food at the Cottage Inn is un-pretentious as well and the menu features a litany of sandwiches and entrées that would have been standards at most eateries across the nation in the 1950s and 60s: burgers, BLTs and clubs; country fried steak, liver and onions, pork chops, spaghetti and meatballs, and Salisbury steak. Popular are the daily lunch specials for $6.99 and the dinner specials at night. On Wednesday and Saturday evenings the special is "All U Care to Eat Fried Chicken" with bread and two sides for $9.99; Monday turkey and dressing, Tuesday roast beef, Thursday meatloaf and Friday salmon patties all come with two sides and bread and cost only $7.99 — these are some of the all-American favorites that make the Cottage Restaurant one of Kentucky's Fabulous Food Finds.

Courthouse Café

127 West Main Street
Whitesburg, Kentucky 41858
(606) 633-5859

Chicken and dumplings are a regular special at the Courthouse Café.

Although this inviting eatery finds itself at the heart of Kentucky coal country, there's more than mountain cooking on the menu at the Courthouse Café. Although some of the local flavors make their way into the kitchen at Laura Schuster and Josephine Richardson's restaurant, diners find a somewhat more sophisticated take on cuisine here, with an emphasis on fresh ingredients and lighter flavors. Depending on the time of year, there might be blackened rainbow trout with steamed vegetables or grilled pork loin with roasted potatoes for dinner and for lunch there are usually daily specials that include "a meat and two" and a vegetarian plate. In addition, there are good burgers, sandwiches, salads and a number of popular dessert items, including the signature Tanglewood Pie. Not named for the western Massachusetts community of the same name, this sweet creation has a layer of blueberries atop a vanilla and cream cheese filling with sliced bananas and whipped cream.

The café, which is housed in a building from 1911, owes its name to its position across the street from the Letcher County Courthouse. Inside quilts and paintings by Kentucky artists adorn the brick walls, and next door sits a gift shop that is also owned by Richardson. Between courses, you can browse the crafts for which Appalachia is famous, but be forewarned: a hand-stitched quilt or whimsically carved wooden rooster might add several hundred dollars to your otherwise modest tab. Not too far away is the Appalshop, a non-profit multidisciplinary arts and education center that produces original films, theater, music, books and more. It's this dedication to Appalachian culture – and the tasty Tanglewood Pie – that make the Courthouse Café one of our Fabulous Food Finds.

Dizzy Whizz

217 West Saint Catherine Street
Louisville, Kentucky 40208
(502) 583-3828

At any given time of day, you'll likely find an interesting cast of characters patronizing the Dizzy Whizz, an old-style neighborhood hamburger joint that opened in 1947 — just steps from the Gothic spires of the majestic Walnut Street Baptist Church on Old Louisville's Millionaires Row. Over the decades, not much has changed at this local landmark surrounded by hundreds of grand Victorian mansions — and this includes the car hops who still deliver the order to your car.

Since there's usually a good size crowd most times of day, it's safe to assume that the food is good, and the prices are fair. In addition to a wide variety of breakfast items served all day long, the Dizzy Whizz offers a good selection of sandwiches and burgers. The main draw, however, is the "Whizzburger," a holdover from the original menu. A regular whizzer — a half-pound version is also available — features two smallish flat-grilled patties sandwiched on a toasted double-decker bun with American cheese, lots of shredded lettuce and zesty dill tartar sauce. It's the perfect match to a side of fries or onion rings and a freshly blended chocolate malt. Other

Try the pork chop biscuit at Dizzy Whizz.

popular choices at the Dizzy Whizz are the Big Fish, a whopping sandwich of breaded cod that is fried crisp but not greasy, and the simple hamburger, which goes for little more than a buck. Good, no-frills drive-in food at the heart of one America's most spectacular historic preservation districts makes Louisville's Dizzy Whizz just one of the neighborhood's Fabulous Food Finds.

Doe Run Inn

500 Doe Run Hotel Road
Brandenburg, Kentucky 40108
(270) 422-2982

Offering authentic regional cooking and hospitality since the 1920s, historic Doe Run Inn boasts what many consider the best fried chicken in the state. The famous Colonel Harland Sanders was even rumored on one occasion to confide that the fried chicken there was better than his own. Former owners Ken and Cherie Whitman claimed that one secret to the juicy chicken's extra crispy crust was the frying it gets in a cast-iron skillet that is 200 years old, which makes it almost as old as the original mill that started it all. Located on a peaceful stream discovered by Squire Boone in 1778, the grounds on which the mill was built became a favorite retreat for those in search of a quiet getaway, and in the first half of the 1900s visitors started renting rooms there. And where there were overnight visitors, there had to be good home cooking.

Meals at today's Doe Run Inn are served family style for parties of four or more, and apart from the fried chicken, favorites include braised beef brisket, hickory smoked pork tenderloin, country

Local staples such as Kentucky beer cheese appear on the menu at Doe Run Inn in Brandenburg, less than an hour's drive from Louisville.

Jim and Opal Green have kept favorites such as beef brisket on the Doe Run Inn menu.

ham with red-eye gravy, and shepherd's pie. Since 2009, Jim and Opal Green have owned the place and the popular all-day, all-you-can-eat comfort-food buffet on Sundays, which features entrée items such as smoked chicken, pulled pork, beef brisket, fried chicken livers, country ham balls, and sides like mashed potatoes, macaroni and cheese, spiced apples, and corn pudding is still a big draw. On Friday nights, seafood lovers enjoy the buffet with frog legs, shrimp cocktail, crab legs, fried fish, oysters, and salmon patties, just to name a few, but the menu is available as well and you can order favorites such as the chicken croquettes or meatloaf platter. For a sweet end to the Doe Run Inn experience, a wide variety of home-baked desserts is available, however the perennial favorite is the lemon chess pie. Flavored with a pinch of coconut, the recipe goes back to the 1950s. Good chess pie, old-fashioned Kentucky favorites and a historic setting make Doe Run Inn one of the most Fabulous Food Finds in the Bluegrass.

Dovie's Restaurant

107 West Fourth Street
Tompkinsville, Kentucky
No telephone

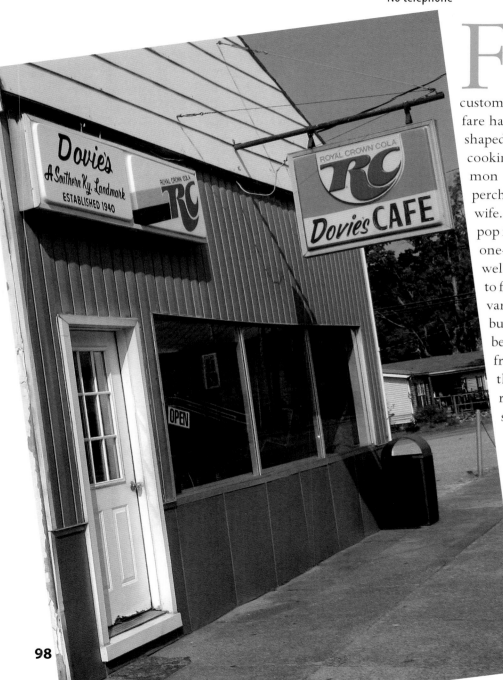

Founded by the Moore family shortly before World War II, Dovie's Restaurant has become a southern Kentucky landmark. Since 1940, customers in search of simple lunch counter fare have crowded around the horseshoe-shaped bar and 26 stools that surround the cooking area, and today it's not uncommon to find a farmer in bib overalls perched next to a businessman or housewife. Even tourists have been known to pop in, since Dovie's reputation for their one-of-a-kind hamburger has spread well beyond the Bluegrass. Their claim to fame, the Dovie Burger is an unusual variation on an American classic: hamburger patties made from fresh ground beef and breadcrumbs that are deep-fried in soybean oil. In a town where the population averages some 3,000 residents, Dovie's has been known to serve more than 1,000 of them in a single day.

Dovie's is still in the Moore family today—before they died, the Moores asked their children to keep the restaurant going—and over the years very little has changed on the menu. It started off with egg sandwiches, fried bologna, hot dogs and their signature hamburgers with special sauce—all served up on a sheet

You've got to love a place that serves up old-fashioned favorites like the humble egg sandwich.

Deep-fried in soybean oil,
Dovie's burgers are one of a kind.

of waxed paper because there are no plates — and that's pretty much what you'll find today. Sandwiches at Dovie's are usually accompanied by coffee or a cola and if you order the Dovie Burger, the counter lady will ask if you want yours "squozed" or "unsquozed," that is with the excess grease squeezed out or not. The Dovie Burger was named best hamburger in the state by *Kentucky Living* magazine in 2005 and not too long after, it was featured on KET's *Kentucky Life* with Dave Shuffet. Dovie's isn't afraid of deep-fat frying and that's why they are one of the state's Fabulous Food Finds.

English Grill at the Brown Hotel

335 South Fourth Street
Louisville, Kentucky 40202
(502) 583-1234

In a modern age of convenience and fast-paced living, Kentucky has always prided itself on its laid-back sense of hospitality and appreciation for the finer things in life. This sense of refinement has been cultivated at Louisville's grand hotels, and the elegant Brown Hotel has enjoyed an especially coveted reputation both for its quiet sophistication and the fine dining in its upscale restaurant, the English Grill.

Restored to its original English Renaissance grandeur, the galleried lobby that leads to the English Grill seems to jump to life from the very silver screens that entertained Depression-weary Louisvillians when the hotel was built in the 1920s. Ornate chandeliers in brass dangle from plaster coffered ceilings accented by graceful arcades decorated in gold leaf and feathery blue scrollwork, and one could easily imagine flappers, gangsters and Jazz-era socialites mingling on the polished marble floors. It is without a doubt one of the most elegant places to eat in the Commonwealth.

Montreal native Laurent Géroli took the helm at the English Grill in 2005, his clean and simple cuisine relying on high-quality local ingredients to artfully create cosmopolitan flavors with regional flair. Popular starters included dishes such as succulent lobster gnocchi with a splash of Basil Hayden bourbon in the pepper sauce and, depending on the season, entrées like a skillet veal chop with caramelized shallots, creamy blue polenta and cubed sweet potatoes would appear on the menu.

In March 2011, however, Matthew Wilcoxson became the chef at the English Grill, and the 25-year-old graduate of the culinary program at Jefferson Community College will be adding his own touches. The menu will still change frequently to make use of the best seasonable ingredients and guests can expect cameos from local flavors in dishes such as Bourbon Barrel smoked salmon with mâche and citrus salad. In addition, he'll keep the hotel's signature dessert on the menu. Known as the "chocolate striptease," the showstopper pairs rich chocolate cake and mousse with hazelnut-crusted chocolate ganache in a flaming orange rum chocolate cup. Treat yourself to an evening at the English Grill and you'll see why many consider it one of the most elegant Fabulous Food Finds in the Commonwealth.

Bourbon Barrel smoked salmon
with mâche salad and
cumin bread.

The Lobby Bar at the uberelegant Brown Hotel is perfect for an afternoon cocktail or a light bite at night.

Fancy Farm Picnic

3131 State Route 399 North
Fancy Farm, Kentucky 42039
No Telephone

34

In 1880 the *Mayfield Monitor* published the following notice: "There will be a barn dance, picnic and 'gander pulling' at Fancy Farm next Thursday. Those that have never seen the latter should turn out on this occasion. It will be interesting." Ever since, the St. Jerome Catholic Church in the small town of Fancy Farm, near Mayfield in Graves County, has hosted its community picnic once a year. Although it started off as a local affair, where people gathered to enjoy regional entertainment and the barbecue made famous in the western part of the state, political candidates at some point began to see the Fancy Farm Picnic as the perfect opportunity to stump for votes. Soon a speaking platform was added, and by the middle of the 20th century, an assuming little picnic had transformed itself into the unofficial kickoff event for the fall election season.

Not only that, in 1985 the *Guinness Book of World Records* recognized the event as the "World's Largest Picnic," a claim to fame that still stands today. In 2008 it was reported that 19,000 pounds

of barbecue, 5,600 pieces of chicken, 750 pounds of potato salad, 160 pounds of lima beans, 140 gallons of corn, 144 pounds of green beans, and 96 pounds of peas had been consumed, not to mention huge quantities of hamburgers, ice cream and sweet tea.

Not surprising, the get-together at Fancy Farm has become a tradition on the Kentucky calendar and it's not uncommon to run into former Fancy Farmers now living on the East or West Coast who faithfully return every year. Volunteers in long huts serve up tons of barbecued pork and mutton, which pit masters have tended and basted since the day before, and attendees wander the grounds, play bingo or join the crowds gathered to cheer — or jeer — the candidates. It only happens once a year, on the first Saturday in August, but the Fancy Farm Picnic is undoubtedly a Kentucky culinary classic, one of its Fabulous Food Finds indeed.

Fava's

159 East Main Street
Georgetown, Kentucky 40324
(502) 863-4383

above right: Regular's have their own coffee cups at Fava's.
below right: Fried pickle chips are a popular side.

Fava's is an old-fashioned soda-fountain kind of place that has been catering to hungry locals since 1910 when Susie and Louie Bertolini Fava opened a confectionery shop in downtown Georgetown. Always jam-packed with friendly locals, the establishment no longer specializes in the mouthwatering ice creams and homemade chocolates concocted by the Favas, but it has maintained a faithful following nonetheless. Today — and several owners later — Fava's still attracts crowds of patrons hungry for a taste of yesteryear with its casual, colorful atmosphere and American diner classics.

Jeni and Howard Gruchow operate Fava's now and they have added their personal touches to the menu, which has grown to more than 100 items and specials today. Aside from the usual suspects such as chicken salad, Ruebens, BLTs, and tuna salad, sandwiches include grilled pimento cheese with tomato, country ham, and po' boys with catfish, roast beef or shrimp. Also available are several burgers, including the giant Fava burger, a half pound of beef charbroiled to order and dressed with lettuce, pickle, onion, mayo and tomato. Sides include popular items such as home fries, onion straws, fried banana peppers, and frickles, tangy slices of crisp-fried pickles.

For supper, guests can choose from entrées like the Clifty Farms country ham dinner, the Kentucky hot brown or the open-faced roast beef sandwich with mashed potatoes and gravy. Friday and Saturday evenings see the addition of dinner favorites such as all-you-can-eat catfish, and fried chicken. For dessert, try a slice of delicious cream or fruit pie or take a whole one home with you. Whatever you get, you're bound to agree that Fava's is one of many Fabulous Food Finds in the state.

Federal Grove
Bed & Breakfast

475 East Main Street
Auburn, Kentucky 42206
(270) 542-6106

At a bed and breakfast inn, you expect to find a good spread in the morning, and Auburn's Federal Grove is no exception. Spend the night in one of the comfortable rooms at the venerable 1871 mansion, and what you wake up to is a taste of the Old South. On your plate you'll find hearty favorites such as country ham, red-eye gravy, biscuits and all the other trimmings that make for a big Kentucky breakfast. But at Federal Grove you're also apt to find something that can't be found at your average bed and breakfast — homemade maple syrup.

Sadly a rarity in affordable eateries today, real mashed potatoes make Wayne and Terry Blythe's bed and breakfast eatery worth the trip.

Said to be the southernmost producer of this sweet delicacy in North America, Federal Grove collects maple sap from mid-January through early March, and then begins the arduous task of boiling it down until it becomes syrup; it takes up to 50 gallons of sap to produce a single gallon of the brown elixir. 100% pure maple syrup is then carefully filtered and bottled in beautiful glass bottles available for sale to the general public.

Fortunately, some of it also finds its way into dishes like the maple-glazed pork chops that are served for lunch and dinner at Federal Grove. Noon is a popular time here, and the sunny back room is often filled with "ladies who lunch" while catching up on the news of the day. In addition to several salads and popular desserts such as the bumble berry cobbler and strawberry cream cake, the lunch menu features a $8.95 "one meat, three sides, and bread" combo that makes you feel like you just sat down at grandma's table. Meats include choices like fried chicken and roast beef and the sides include ham-seasoned green beans, fried corn, baked apples and real mashed potatoes glistening with butter. Because they have some of the best, buttteriest mashed potatoes around and because you can't beat the Kentucky maple syrup, Federal Grove is one Kentucky's Fabulous Food Find.

Ferrell's Hamburgers

1001 South Main Street
Hopkinsville, Kentucky 42240
(270) 886-1445

opkinsville is known as the home of Edgar Cayce, the Sleeping Prophet, and it was also a stop on the infamous Trail of Tears. It's known as well for Ferrell's Hamburgers, a tiny, downtown diner that opened in 1929. With its late hours and proximity to Fort Campbell, it's a popular hangout for night owls and has become something of a local landmark. In August of 1955 it was a gathering spot when the national news reported that aliens had landed on a nearby farm and provoked a shoot out with local residents.

Ferrell's has changed very little over the years, and this includes the no-frills menu, which offers a simple line up of burgers, sandwiches, pecan pie and chili. The chili, a perfect accompaniment to an old-fashioned fried egg sandwich, is pleasantly mild and has an almost creamy mouth feel. The basic hamburger costs only $1.70 and when you put in your

order Doris Ferrell trots out from the back room, reaches into a cooler under the front counter for a small ball of ground beef and uses a metal spatula to pound it into submission before throwing it on the griddle. Since Ferrell's is open 24 hours a day, breakfast is a major feature and diners can have eggs to order, toast, bacon, sausage and ham as well. The menu's small, but the history is big at Ferrell's — and they never close! — so

A simple diner lunch: a bowl of homemade chili and a fried egg sandwich.

this is why this Hopkinsville icon is one of Kentucky's most cherished Fabulous Food Finds.

Frances Bar-B-Q

418 East Fourth
Tompkinsville, Kentucky 42167
(270) 487-8550

When Frances burned to the ground in April of 2009, the residents of Monroe County feared that more than 30 years of tradition had come to an end. But, fortunately for fans of 'cue, David Arms relocated and quickly reopened the restaurant his parents started back when he was a younger man. Today, during a typical work week, it's not uncommon for him and his wife Jennifer to go through more than 10,000 pounds of shoulder steak, the restaurant's biggest seller. Sliced thin and cooked over a bed of coals, the meat has a grilled smokiness that goes well with a good slathering of tangy, peppery tomato barbeque sauce that has been given a heavy-handed dose of vinegar. Talk to the locals and they'll tell you the stuff is addictive.

The secret to the sauce is a family recipe that goes back some 100 years and Arms markets it with some help from his friend, country music star John Anderson. It's available at certain grocery chains in the region and at the restaurant, of course, where it's gobbled up with plates of shredded pork, beef brisket, pork ribs or grilled chicken. The sauce is so tasty that Arms even put it to use on hard-cooked eggs. Really a variation on the pickled egg, barbecued eggs offer an unusual taste that has become a specialty in the area.

At only 60 cents, a barbecued egg is a nice topper on the "Mix Plate" featuring any three meats, which includes ham, pork chops and even hot dogs. Because it's the reported birth place of the barbecued egg and because the shoulder steak is first rate, Frances Bar-B-Q is one of many Fabulous Food Finds in Kentucky.

David Arms specializes in barbecue, but the fried catfish is good, too.

Frances' Diner

1315 Combs Road
Hazard, Kentucky 41701
(606) 436-0090

Y ou've got to love a place that's open 24 hours a day – particularly when the food's good and the wait-resses are friendly. But, unfortunately, never-close eateries seem to be a thing of the past and it's hard to find them nowadays, especially in smaller towns. In eastern Kentucky, however, there are several diners open for night owls in search of down-home cooking and service with a smile, and one of them is Frances' Diner in Hazard. Frances Napier opened the current restaurant in 1990 – the two decades before, she had another place right around the corner – and since then she's become something of a local icon, an old friend to generations of patrons.

Each day sees a changing selection of nearly twenty items. In addition to stan-dards like mashed potatoes, home fries, macaroni and cheese, buttered corn and cole slaw, choices include fried okra, mustard greens, fried apples, brown beans, sweet potatoes, fried cabbage, and macaroni and tomatoes. There's even potato cakes – and deviled eggs, that most

Frances' or France's Diner — however you spell it, old-fashioned fare like fried chicken livers and gravy and butterscotch pie is on the menu.

hard-to-find of all diner delicacies.

Practically everything is homemade at Frances' Diner, from brown beans and chili to the meringue pies in the rotating cooler behind the counter. And get this, they even do real mashed potatoes and not those awful instant things that so many lower-end restaurants do nowadays. It's open 24 hours a day and they serve real mashed potatoes — that's enough to make Frances' Diner a Fabulous Food Find in my book.

Garrett's Restaurant

215 North Broadway
Carlisle, Kentucky 40311
(859) 289-7582

George and Becky Garrett have operated their namesake eatery from a simple white storefront on Carlisle's charming main square for more than 40 years. Like the establishment itself, the menu is small in size, but what it lacks in selection it more than makes up for in flavor. For breakfast you'll find the usual lineup – a variety of eggs, omelets, and pancakes with all the accoutrements – and at lunch there's a dozen or so burgers and sandwiches, in addition to sides and the lunch plate, the restaurant's biggest draw. For just $6.25 you get your choice of roast beef, city ham, fish, baked country ham or country fried steak with choice of bread and three different accompaniments, which include brown beans, potato salad, cole slaw and apple sauce, just to name a few. A dry-erase board touts a daily special as well, and if you're lucky it'll be the delicious fried chicken, which offers a juicy breast portion often served with sliced tomatoes, green beans and mashed potatoes and gravy.

Country-fried steak and perfectly seasoned fried chicken – two favorites at Garrett's Restaurant in Carlisle.

One of the best parts of a visit to Garrett's is a stroll around the town square after your meal. Although the restaurant itself is somewhat plain on the inside, the view outside the front window is worth a visit alone. Dominated by a Victorian courthouse, much of village center remains unchanged, offering a glimpse of what the town must have looked like a hundred years ago. Not only that, small-town America is alive and well here and the friendly locals will make you feel at home when you walk through the doors at Garrett's. It's the friendly people, combined with the great lunch specials and main square location, that make Garrett's one of Kentucky's Fabulous Food Finds.

Granny's Kitchen

216 Market Square
Russellville, Kentucky 42276
(270) 726-7071

Although James C. Whittinghill has owned it since 2003, Granny's Kitchen has been a popular hangout with southern cooking fans of all ages since its doors opened years ago in Russellville. In the afternoon, it's a popular hangout for high school students who turn up to chat with friends and order the best cheeseburgers in town; in the morning, old-timers show up to sit at their regular table and start the day with a hot cup of coffee. No matter what the time of day, the food is good and it seems there's always a smiling waitress waiting to take your order.

above: For a hearty side try Granny's hash browns with a variety of toppings. below: A great way to start the day: steak, bacon or tenderloin biscuits.

For plate lunches there's a beef Manhattan or beans with cornbread, and dinners, served with two sides and bread, include favorites such as fried catfish, sliced country ham and country fried steak smothered in white gravy. But if it's not lunch or dinner you're looking for, order something for breakfast, which starts at 5:00 a.m. and is served all day long. Apart from a selection of breakfast specials, omelets, and homemade pancakes, the menu features a "build your own" section with eggs cooked to order, as well as bacon, sausage, tenderloin, home fries, and sliced tomatoes, among others. There's also a choice of shredded hash browns topped with any combination of cheese, gravy, grilled mushrooms, ham, roast beef, sausage, bacon or chopped onion, tomato, and pepper. But, for a taste of Granny's star item, try one, two, or three of the breakfast biscuits made from scratch every morning—they come filled with fried egg, cheese, pork loin, bacon, sausage patties, chicken, steak or country ham. It's the wide variety of homemade biscuits that makes Granny's Kitchen one of my favorite Fabulous Food Finds.

123

Green Derby Restaurant

846 York Street
Newport, Kentucky 41071
(859) 431-8740

A northern Kentucky favorite, the Green Derby has been making people feel at home since its doors opened over 60 years ago. According to former owner John Haller, whose grandparents opened the neighborhood watering hole on a quiet Newport street in 1947, the Green Derby started off "as a bar with some small-time gambling." His grandmother, Mollie McCann, began supplying food for the patrons from her small kitchen and in 1957 it was enlarged and a dining room added on. The McCann's tavern quickly became known for its welcoming atmosphere and home cooking.

Decades later, the Green Derby is still known for good burgers, steaks, pork chops and seafood dinners, but it's the fish sandwich that has made it famous. Repeatedly voted the best in the tri-state by readers of the *Cincinnati Post*, the fried halibut sandwich comes from Haller's mother Helen Cummins, the woman he credits as the culinary foundation of the restaurant. The

A favorite in Cincinnati: the fish sandwich at Newport's Green Derby.

"favorite" Derby salad, a hot, slaw-like concoction of shredded iceberg lettuce and chopped onion served with hot bacon dressing, was her creation as well. Like the mett sausages and sauerkraut on the menu, it's popular with the large concentration of German-Americans in the Cincinnati area.

In June of 2009 John Haller's family decided to close up shop, but luckily for many loyal patrons, the restaurant did not sit dormant for long. Several months later, Tom Cardosi and the Hosea family reopened the restaurant. Although some renovations would come to the interior, they stayed true to the original menu and are still attracting crowds today. Give the Green Derby a try and you'll see why their fish sandwich and the hot slaw are two of Kentucky's Fabulous Food Finds.

Greyhound Tavern

When the server brings your order at the Greyhound Tavern, you quickly realize they don't do things small at this, northern Kentucky's oldest continuously operating restaurant. The perfectly fried banana pepper rings, for example, come mounded high on a small platter with a side of creamy horseradish sauce; the signature onion rings are so large — most cannot even eat an entire order by themselves — that a single one fits on a small plate and you need a fork and knife to eat it. You can even order them stuffed with a blend of shrimp and herbed cream cheese and a side of sweet tomato relish.

The menu at the Greyhound leans toward the traditional, and the folks there have been serving up signature dishes since 1921, when Johnny Hauer started an ice cream parlor at what was then the end of the line for local streetcars before they turned around and headed back across the river to Cincinnati. After a man by the name of Al Frisch bought the eatery and renamed it the Greyhound Grill in honor of his dog trainer brother, the restaurant expanded its menu and it became the Fort Mitchell hotspot for double-decker burgers, steaks and chops that it is today. Some other crowd pleasers include the fried chicken, the walleye pike and the pecan-crusted chicken with Maker's Mark sauce for entrées and Butch's bean soup or the beer cheese with pretzel bread for starters. A house specialty is the

Kentucky hot slaw, cabbage sliced super thin and doused with a hot sweet-and-sour dressing topped off with chunks of fried jowl bacon. Readers of *Kentucky Monthly* magazine selected the Greyhound Tavern as the best restaurant in northern Kentucky, but give it a try and discover for yourself why it's one of the Fabulous Food Finds in the whole state.

above: A simple country ham sandwich makes a nice lunch at the Greyhound Tavern. right: Fried banana pepper rings are a popular sharing item.

129

Hall's on the River

1225 Athens-Boonesboro Road
Winchester, Kentucky 40391
(859) 527-6620

A trip on the old Athens Road is a ride through history. Home to the largest collection of dry masonry stone fences in the nation today, this part of the Bluegrass was Daniel Boone country, and visible reminders still remain more than two centuries after the famous frontiersman blazed the trail through the Cumberland Gap. Reconstructed Fort Boonesborough keeps the pioneer spirit alive, but it counts as only one of several hidden treasures in the area today. Just a mile or so downstream is Hall's on the River, a secluded getaway that has people driving long distances for a slice of Bluegrass culinary history.

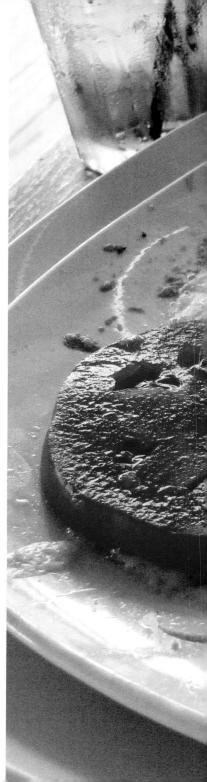

Karl Crase and Jesse Abrams have owned the Winchester restaurant since 2000, but diners have been coming ever since George and Gertrude Hall started it around 1965. The focal point of Hall's is a spacious deck overlooking the green-brown waters of the Kentucky, however, five interior fireplaces make Hall's on the River just as inviting in the dead of winter as during the dog days of summer.

A popular starters at Hall's is the specialty known as beer cheese, a tangy blend of sharp Cheddar, beer and spices served with crackers and crudité. Its prominence is hardly surprising given that John Allman, the brainchild behind the snack, popularized it at a legendary restaurant he opened across the road in the 1930s. But if beer cheese is not your thing, try the fried banana peppers, another culinary legacy of the Allman era. Oysters on the half shell, chilled shrimp, deep-fried, bacon-wrapped oysters and a variety of reasonably priced American pub snacks are available as well.

As would be expected, items such as frog legs and fried catfish make up a large portion of the entrée selections, but steaks and pasta are popular as well. Favorites like the country ham with red-eye gravy and chicken livers with smashed potatoes add a touch of Kentucky comfort food to the menu, a sizeable list of offerings whose Bluegrass lineage is rounded out with lamb fries, the Nicholasville-inspired delicacy popular with more intrepid diners. A recent addition to the lineup is the seafood hot brown, a luscious version of the Louisville original — and that's why it counts as one of the 111 Fabulous Food Finds in Kentucky.

The seafood hot brown – a delicious take on the Louisville original.

Harper's Catfish

3085 Old Gallatin Road
Scottsville, Kentucky 42164
(270) 622-7557

45

Kentucky has a number of eateries known for catfish, but ask the natives who has the very best and chances are one name will keep popping up: Harper's Catfish. Their specialty shows up in the name, so that shows you they take their fish very seriously here. In fact, it's even been said by quite a few that Harper's has the best catfish this side of the Mississippi; ask anyone waiting in the lines that form outside the door Friday and Saturday nights and they'll tell you as much. The portions are large and inexpensive, and the catfish nuggets are moist and flavorful with a perfectly fried cornmeal crust that is light and crispy. Paired with an order of crunchy crinkle-cut fries and Harper's famous sweet slaw – they make gallons of it each day – this catfish is so good it will make a true southerner blush. The hushpuppies are good, too.

A popular stop with locals and vacationers at nearby Barren Lake, Harper's has been serving up its famous catfish in its 200-seat restaurant since 1978. "It's a simple, no-frills kind of place that is popular with local families," says friendly server Stephanie Russell, "but we have people drive here from as far away as Illinois."

But there is more than just catfish on the menu at Harper's and three meals a day are served. For breakfast there are eggs cooked to order, country ham and pancakes, just to name a few. In addition to other seafood items like shrimp, clams, oysters and frog legs, customers will find a variety of standards such as chicken, chops, steaks and burgers plated up in a simple concrete block building at the end of a two-level parking lot. It's not a fancy place, but the catfish is good and cheap, and that earns it a spot as one of the Fabulous Food Finds in my book.

The décor at Harper's is plain, but you won't notice the surroundings when you taste the catfish.

Hih Burger

413 South Fourth Street
Murray, Kentucky 42071
(270) 753-1155

right: Chicken and dressing is a regular choice with the Hih Burger lunch crowd.

In Murray the bright blue and yellow sign in front of the Hih Burger restaurant has been a beacon for fans of good diner food for more than half a century. It's an un-fancy place that seats about 80 at a number of booths, some Formica-topped tables and counter stools, but the no-frills atmosphere doesn't seem to bother the crowds of hungry patrons that start coming through the doors when they open at 5:00 six mornings a week. According to Larry Roberson, the previous owner whose parents started the restaurant in 1957 and modeled it after a diner they had visited in Michigan, the friendly service and down-home flavors quickly made it a popular hangout with the locals. Although the name officially changed from Roberson's to Renfroe's Hih Burger not too long ago, the tradition of simple food and quick

service still survives today.

Aside from hearty breakfast items that include fluffy, homemade pancakes and from-scratch biscuits with creamy milk gravy, Hih Burger is known for its wide assortment of burgers and sandwiches. But it's the affordable weekly lunch specials featuring "a meat and three" that have garnered the diner much of its fame. Pork barbecue, chicken and dressing, and roast beef are standards, and the choice of sides includes broccoli salad, candied yams, cranberry sauce, cucumber and onion salad, deviled eggs and white beans. There's also a fish special with one, two or three pieces of fried fish with french fries, white beans and slaw that packs the place on Fridays, when they stay open till 8:00 p.m. Normally, they close at 2:00 p.m. every day, but because they know how to serve up a mean breakfast and a good lunch, Hih Burger is one of western Kentucky's Fabulous Food Finds.

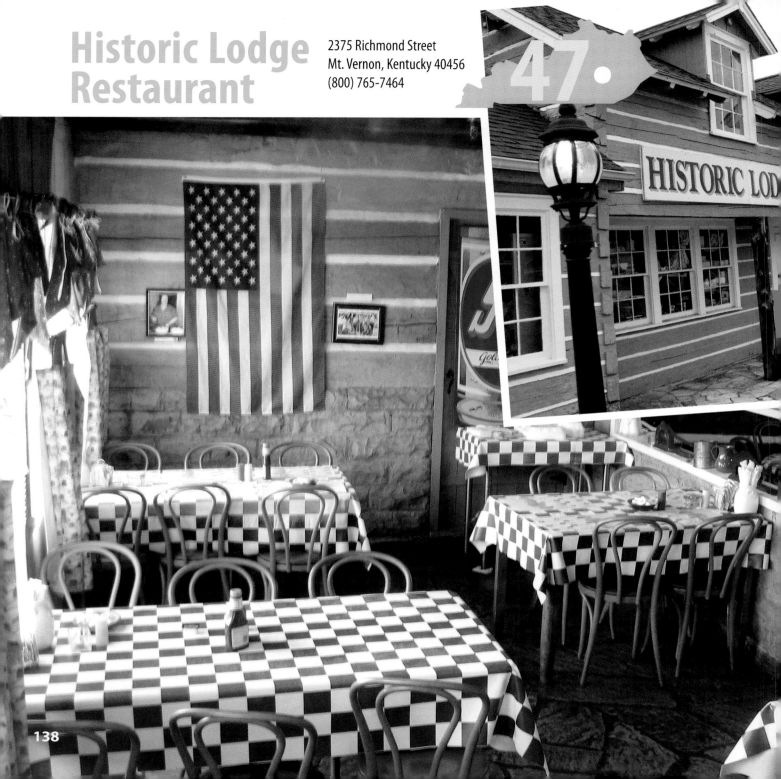

Historic Lodge
Restaurant

2375 Richmond Street
Mt. Vernon, Kentucky 40456
(800) 765-7464

47

HISTORIC LODGE

Located in central Kentucky, in Rockcastle County, the Renfro Valley has become a Mecca for fans of country and bluegrass music over the years. Every June it hosts a popular music festival and it is also home to the Kentucky Music Hall of Fame, a museum which honors performers, songwriters, publishers, managers, comedians and other professionals who have made significant contributions to the music industry in Kentucky and around the world. It's also known for the Historic Lodge Restaurant, a roadside eatery that has been serving up "boardin' house suppers" and "country fixin's" since 1939.

Today, this rustic hideaway is just a stone's throw from the traffic of bustling I-75 and it makes for an easy layover before or after one of the many live music shows that keep Renfro Valley hopping with activity most of the year. To find out who is on stage, just take a look at the list of acts displayed in the menu.

Aside from stick-to-your-ribs breakfast items such as omelets, fried apples, grits, and buttermilk biscuits and gravy, you'll find dinner fare focusing on country cooking favorites at the Historic Lodge Restaurant. Sugar-cured ham, fried chicken, pork chops and homemade meatloaf are just some of the specialties that make regular appearances at the table. Lunch is a popular meal here and $7.99 gets you the noon special which features a main course such as chicken and dumplings, chicken livers or country fried steak with two sides and rolls or corn bread. Just like the music that has made Renfro Valley famous, the fare at the Historic Lodge Restaurant is down-home and simple — and that's what makes it one of our Fabulous Food Finds in Kentucky.

Holly Hill Inn

426 North Winter Street
Midway, Kentucky 40347
(859) 846-4732

At a bucolic hilltop hideaway not far from downtown Midway, you'll find one of the most pleasant dining experiences in the Bluegrass. It's known as the Holly Hill Inn and owners Ouita and Chris Michel have made a name for their restaurant both inside and outside the Bluegrass. Their numerous accolades include the description as "a gem of a restaurant" by *The New York Times.*

Nestled at the crossroads of the Leestown and Georgetown roads, the picturesque grounds of today's Holly Hill Inn were home to an early tavern that was replaced by the current handsome Greek Revival structure sometime in the 1840s. After subsequent modifications and several different occupants, including the Parrishes, who took up residence in 1903, the country manor was converted into an inn in 1979. The Michels, both alums of the Culinary Institute of America, took over in 2000, with Ouita working her

Silver dollar biscuits with country ham are a wonderful start to Sunday brunch at Chris and Ouita Michel's hilltop retreat.

magic in the kitchen and Chris showing off his skills as sommelier and host.

The result is a welcoming retreat with friendly, attentive service and a kitchen team dedicated to community farm-based cuisine that features imaginative dishes paying tribute to Kentucky's rich tradition of cooking. Although a modern, continental flare for entertaining characterizes the overall experience at Holly Hill Inn, the flavors come straight from the Bluegrass. Names on the menu such as Waterworks Farm, Weisenberger Mills, and Duncan Ranch ensure that the menu has a steady supply of farm-fresh products and artisanal goodies.

Holly Hill Inn is open for lunch and dinner five days a week and the menu changes with the seasons to make use of the best local produce. For lunch or dinner you'll find tempting selections such as baby spoon bread and lobster soufflé, Sheltowee mushroom turnovers, crab quiche, or Stone Cross ham steak and cheese grits. The popular prix-fixe Sunday brunch features choices such as shrimp and grits, pecan-dusted trout with browned butter sauce and eggs sardou served atop a toasted English muffin with artichoke bottoms and lemony hollandaise. Whatever your choice, a meal at Holly Hill Inn will be a treat and you'll agree that it's one of the most Fabulous Food Finds anywhere.

Horseshoe Steakhouse

2112 Fort Campbell Boulevard
Hopkinsville, Kentucky 42240
(270) 886-7734

49

When you're heading out of Hopkinsville on Ft. Campbell Boulevard, don't blink or you might miss the Horseshoe Steakhouse. Open since 1968, it's a small place that seats just 64, but ask any of the locals who belly up to the counter and they'll tell you the Horseshoe is big on flavor. In addition, the portions are generous and the service is friendly and unhurried. That's why it's one of western Kentucky's Fabulous Food Finds.

As can be imagined, steaks are big at the Horseshoe, and the selection of beef is classic supper club fare from the 60s and 70s. In addition to T-bones and strips, there's a popular 32-ounce super sirloin for two, not to mention an 8-ounce filet and a juicy rib-eye sandwich served on a toasted bun with fresh tomato slices, onion and crisp lettuce. There's even a steak salad, and the locals will tell you the half-pound horseshoe cheeseburger is as good as any you'll get.

Despite the predominance of red meat on the menu, guests at the Horseshoe will also find chicken, pork and seafood selections, not to mention a good number of salads and sides. Ask what to order with your hamburger steak or grilled chicken, and smiling workers like Faye Allen will tell you the hash browns are the hands-down favorite. Seasoned with chopped onion and

paprika, they're fried on the grill till per-fectly crispy and delicious. Give them a try with one of the classic steaks and see why the Horseshoe is a no-frills local institution.

Hutchen's Drive In

601 North Main Street
Benton, Kentucky 42025
(270) 527-9424

The small-town diner is a thing of the past in many towns across the country, however, the Bluegrass has its fair share.

A western Kentucky favorite is Hutchen's Drive In, which opened in 1947, when W.C. Hutchens purchased a building in downtown Benton and opened a new restaurant. The coffee was always hot and fresh, and the unpretentious menu quickly won a faithful following with its assortment of sandwiches, burgers, fountain drinks, hot dogs, and milkshakes. Since then the eatery has grown into a full-service dining experience and today owners Kevin and Rhonda Knees still value the importance of taste, good service, and hospitality.

The menu at Hutchens offers nearly 20 different sandwiches, which run the gamut from traditional burgers and hot dogs to fried catfish and Philly cheese steak. The hot ham and cheese continues to be a favorite after all these years, as does the patty melt, however, most seem to prefer the barbecue pork and turkey, which are served on large

white buns that have been pressed and toasted, panini-style. Dinners, like the hamburger steak with onions, catfish filets, ribs and marinated sirloin steak, come with Texas toast and a choice of potato, salad or three vegetables. Sides include breaded squash, potato salad, and pigtail fries, and for coleslaw fans, there are both vinegar and mayo varieties.

Breakfast at Hutchens is a big event as well, and among the rib-sticking favorites is the country ham special with two eggs cooked to order and a huge slice of meat with biscuits and gravy or toast and hash browns. The big Hutch includes two pancakes, bacon or sausage, three cooked-to-order eggs and hash browns with toast or biscuits and gravy. They've kept the American diner experience alive since 1947, and that's why Hutchen's Drive In is one of my Fabulous Food Finds.

For something different, try the barbecued turkey sandwich at Hutchen's.

Hutchison's Grocery

1201 Second Street
Maysville, Kentucky 41056
(606) 564-3797

In today's world of bustling chain supermarkets and impersonal megastores, Hutchison's Grocery is one of those rare places that have withstood the passage of time. It's the typical general store your grandparents would have frequented, and this one has been in continuous operation for some 160 years. Instead of sprawling aisles, bright neon lights and cookie-cutter architecture, patrons of this Maysville landmark find small crowded spaces, cluttered shelves — and an old butcher's block near the front door. There's also a large cooler for soft drinks and a tall cabinet used for hanging country hams, one of the store's biggest draws.

Cissy Lester, the store's owner, has worked

Around for 160 years, Hutchison's is still going strong today. It's the place to come for simple sandwiches in Maysville.

there since she was a teenager, and every year she ships hundred of hams throughout the country. A former customer was Maysville's most famous daughter, Rosemary Clooney, who frequented the store as a young child and had hams shipped to her in California after achieving stardom. Part of her job today involves the preparation of the old-fashioned sandwiches that have become the hallmark of a visit to Hutchison's. In addition to what Cissy calls "the best burgers in town," people love the fried bologna, pepper loaf and "city ham" sandwiches, but as can be expected, it's the country ham that many people come for. Served on plain white bread, they're best with a bit of mayonnaise, some lettuce and a slice of tomato and onion. Because you don't find many old-fashioned general stores nowadays, much less those that make you a sandwich to order, Hutchison's Grocery in one of the state's Fabulous Food Finds indeed.

J. Graham's Café at the Brown Hotel

335 South Fourth Street
Louisville, Kentucky 40202
(502) 583-1234

52

Regally perched at the corner of Broadway and Fourth Street in downtown Louisville, the 16-story Brown Hotel anchors the south end of the city's old entertainment district. Back in the 1920s, majestic theaters and grand movie palaces dotted the area, and it was here that wealthy lumber mogul J. Graham Brown spent a whopping $4 million to construct a state-of-the-art facility. Completed in 1923, the hotel quickly assumed the role as the city's social and business center, and it served as a bastion for local artists and intelligentsia during the bleak years of Prohibition. Despite the devastating flood of 1937 and a period when the hotel closed and threatened to breathe its last, the Brown survives today as a shining example of a community's undying connection to its past.

Part of this history is the creation of one of the state's most famous dishes, a luscious sandwich that stars on the menu at J. Graham's Café. The story be-

Photo by John Nation

hind it goes back to the 1920s, when the Brown Hotel drew over 1,200 guests each evening for its popular dinner dance. Tired after hours of dancing, revelers would retire to the restaurant for a bite to eat in the wee hours of the morning, but they soon grew tired of the traditional ham and eggs. To tempt his guests' palates,

150

*The Brown Hotel is the place
to get the one and only original hot brown.*

chef Fred Schmidt set out to create something new and thus was born the hot brown, an open-faced turkey sandwich with bacon and a delicate, cheesy Mornay sauce. Over the years, many takes on the hot brown have appeared at eateries throughout Kentucky, however, the Brown Hotel remains the place to come for the original, where it's served in a ceramic skillet.

Apart from this storied creation, J. Graham's offers guests a bistro-style option for casual hotel dining with an emphasis on fresh local produce. Open daily from 7:00 a.m. to 2:00 p.m., the café offers a contemporary à la carte menu as well as an express lunch buffet or a full luncheon buffet option that includes a decadent dessert display as well as salads, entrées and gourmet soups such as French onion with a Gruyere crouton. It's also the place to get a slice of original Derby Pie, the chocolate and nut confection from Kern's Kitchen that has been a local favorite with sweet teeth since 1954. Because it's the birthplace of the hot brown, head on over to this Louisville landmark and see why it's one of our Fabulous Food Finds.

The lunch buffet at J. Graham's features a variety of fresh salads and sides.

Photo by Stacy Duncan

Joe's Older than Dirt

8131 New LaGrange Road
Louisville, Kentucky 40222
(502) 426-2074

53

When you spy the beat-up old moose out in front of the tidy white bar in Louisville's Lyndon neighborhood, you'll know you've found Joe's Older than Dirt. Serving up good times and good food since 1937, when Joe Keal fulfilled his dream of opening a tavern for local railway patrons, this Derby City classic has become a haven for serious beer drinkers. A wide variety of beers are on tap, and beer's the perfect accompaniment to one of Joe's most famous menu items, the fried bologna sandwich. Slightly charred on the griddle, it's then topped with fried onions and served on a toasted bun with homemade potato chips. In addition to great sandwiches such as the Reuben, grilled bacon and cheese, and the belly-bustin' fish sandwich, you'll find a good selections of salads and appetizers as well.

Over the years, Joe's has grown to accommodate an expanding clientele and today there is all-season outdoor seating with an inviting atmosphere. With its rough-hewn wood

It's pure beef but they call it the mooseburger, no doubt because of its size – and the mascot out front.

and rustic feel, Joe's can make people forget they're in Kentucky and reminds one of being in a lodge in northern Michigan or Wisconsin. Because this is the place to go for some of the best pub grub in the Bluegrass State, Joe's is one of my Fabulous Food Finds.

left: The fried baloney sandwich – classic Kentucky pub grub.

Jonathan at Gratz Park

120 West Second Street
Lexington, Kentucky 40507
(859) 252-4949

Located within the historic Gratz Park Inn, Jonathan Lundy's stylish restaurant has been a Bluegrass favorite since he and his wife Cara opened it in 1998. A graduate of Johnson and Wales University, Lundy's pedigree is steeped in Kentucky history — his great, great, great grandfather was the founder of Calumet Baking Powder Company and also established Calumet Farm, a thoroughbred dynasty that produced a number of legendary racehorses — and the menu reflects it.

Innovative dishes pay homage to regional influences with sometimes whimsical takes on Kentucky classics, and seasonal inspiration comes from local farmers and producers. Popular starters often include selections such as Ale-8-One braised pork belly with crystallized ginger-shallot confit and pimento cheese grit fries, served with banana pepper mayo and green tomato piccalilli.

There might also be something like a Pike Valley Farms deviled egg trio (country ham, asparagus-chive, and smoked

Photo by Lee Th

The sea scallop hot brown is a signature appetizer at Jonathan Lundy's restaurant.
Get the recipe in his cookbook Jonathan's Bluegrass Table.

salmon) or king crab benedictine, an interesting arrangement of corn bread crackers topped with cream cheese cucumber spread and crab meat. A favorite is the sea scallop hot brown, a clever take on the Derby City original with rounds of toasted brioche crowned with halves of fresh scallops and broiled with country ham, tomato and bacon before receiving a drizzle of flavorful shellfish-infused cream sauce. The only problem with this dish is that you might just decide to order another helping instead of moving on to your next course. The sea scallop hot brown is just one of the many things that makes Jonathan one of my favorite Fabulous Food Finds in Kentucky.

Jot 'Em Down Store

3299 Russell Cave Road
Lexington, Kentucky 40511
(859) 299-5889

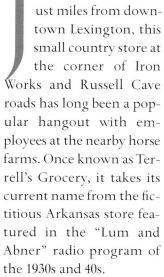

55

Just miles from downtown Lexington, this small country store at the corner of Iron Works and Russell Cave roads has long been a popular hangout with employees at the nearby horse farms. Once known as Terrell's Grocery, it takes its current name from the fictitious Arkansas store featured in the "Lum and Abner" radio program of the 1930s and 40s.

Lum and Abner? Most people today don't have a clue who they were, but somewhere in the recesses of the American subconscious are two gentlemen from the Ouachita Mountains of Arkansas who were superstars in their day. Better known as Lum and Abner, their real names were Chet Lauck and Tuffy Goff, and given their relative obscurity today, it's hard to convey just how popular they were back then. Their career spanned almost 25

Tired of the same old burger? Try the hot mett sandwich at Jot 'em Down Store.

years and their influence on popular culture lives on today, whether you realize it or not. When you hear Jed Clampett say, "Eee doggies" on the *Beverly Hillbillies,* you're hearing an echo of Abner Peabody and if you've seen *Green Acres, Petticoat Junction,* the *Andy Griffith Show* or *Hee Haw,* you've seen characters shaped by Lum and Abner's humor. In fact, it wouldn't be too much of a stretch to say that the modern stereotype of the hillbilly was firmly set in the national consciousness by their radio show.

Robert Terrell remembered his father and uncle in the store in the 1930s, faithfully listening to the show every night, and says it wasn't long before customers started calling them Lum and Abner. Hearing about the inadvertent copycats on a horse-buying trip to the Bluegrass, the real characters stopped in one day to say hello and gave them a sign that read Jot 'em Down Store. ("Jot 'em down" refers to the practice of extending credit.) The rest is, as they say, history.

Stop in for a boloney sandwich and an Ale-8-One today and somewhere around the store you'll most likely see Robert "Robey" Terrell II, who took over after his father died in 1998. He's often behind the deli counter in the back, wrapping up sandwiches for stable hands, trainers and anyone else who stops by for a quick bite. The selection is simple and consists of standards like pimento cheese, boloney and cheese and hot metts. Hot metts are spicy links of smoked German sausage links made of pork and beef that are grilled and served atop a roll with mustard and onion. The hot metts are some of the best around and that, combined with an interesting background story, makes Jot 'em Down Store a Fabulous Food Find.

Juanita's Burger Boy

1450 South Brook Street
Louisville, Kentucky 40208
(502) 635-7410

56

Although Juanita left a couple of years ago — she operated the small storefront since 1980, garnering it a reputation as the neighborhood's quintessential greasy spoon — locals still know it as Juanita's Burger Boy. Located at the corner of Burnett and Brook streets, where the edges of Old Louisville fade into the University of Louisville's main campus, it was Orthober's Market back in the 1930s and became Greg's Place diner in the 1960s. It quickly developed a reputation as a dive where late-night revelers and cramming U of L students could pop in at any hour for a cheap bite and a decent cup of coffee.

When Dan and R.J. Borsch took over in July 2008, the brothers started by giving the place a good scrubbing; after that they took down the plywood from the windows to let in more light and repainted the interior in bright shades of tomato soup. Fortunately, they didn't fiddle around with the menu too much, sticking with a modestly priced selection of burgers, sandwiches and plate-lunch dinners, as well as the famous all-day breakfasts. In addition to pancakes, French toast and omelets, there are hearty breakfasts with eggs, country fried steak, biscuits with gravy, and more. One of the most popular choices with hungry U of L students is the big man special, which

Just steps from the campus of the University of Louisville, Juanita's Burger Boy is a 24-hour favorite with Cardinals fans.

gets you two biscuits smothered in gravy, along with a couple of eggs cooked to order, home fries, toast and choice of ham, sausage or bacon – all for just $5.99.

Even though you'll find T-bone steaks, rib-eye sandwiches, grilled cheese, pork chops, fried fish, patty melts and lots of different sides, Juanita's is rightfully known for its burgers. Whatever you order, chances are you'll run across a colorful character or two at Juanita's, especially the later it gets. With its reputation as a hotspot for the after-hours bar crowd and students looking for a late-night snack, there's usually a steady stream of interesting types during the wee hours. That's one of the reason's Juanita's is one of the best 24-hour Fabulous Food Finds for U of L fans.

Judy's Castle

1302 31 West By Pass
Bowling Green, Kentucky 42101
(270) 842-8736

The slogan at this Bowling Green landmark is "no hassle at the Castle" — the reason being that the friendly staff will go out of its way to accommodate special orders here. Most of the guests, however, are more than happy to stick with menu items as they're prepared because if the restaurant's been around for more than 40 years they must be doing something right in the food department. According to Paul Durbin, who along with his wife took over the restaurant in 1994, this success is due in no small part to a no-nonsense approach to simple American staples and the eatery's friendly atmosphere. Saturdays the place is often packed with breakfast and lunch regulars — you'll usually find a good weekday crowd as well — but there always seems to be a free table or two so don't let that stop you from popping in for breakfast, lunch or dinner at Judy's Castle.

Open the menu and aside from sandwiches you'll find affordable standards such as roast beef and gravy, broasted chicken, pork chops, country ham and chicken livers during the afternoon and evening, not to mention a wide assortment of breakfast dishes, which are served all day long. For a taste of the local favorite, try the country fried steak, which appears in several incarnations on the menu. Not only can you get it with a choice of three sides as a dinner, for a little over $4, you can get it paired with two eggs and biscuits and gravy or else you can enjoy it atop a single biscuit for about half the price.

Whatever you get, make sure to save room for some of Judy's signature pie.

Chocolate, pecan and peanut butter are popular flavors, but you can't go wrong with the sweet coconut cream topped with four inches of fluffy meringue. Because it's got great daily plate lunch specials and wonderful meringue pies, Judy's Castle is one of many Fabulous Food Finds in the southern part of the Commonwealth.

Kilbern's at the Campbell House

1375 South Broadway
Lexington, Kentucky 40504
(859) 255-4281

58

Kentucky beer cheese is a good start to any meal.

Everyone has heard of the Ford Motor Company, the great American success story that started up in 1903 and two decades later would be producing nine out of 10 cars on the road. Most people, however, don't know that at one time Ford was almost as well known for its recipes as it was for its rides. From 1908 to 1996, the Ford Motor Company published a magazine known as the *Ford Times* that featured a regular selection of recipes from popular roadside restaurants. These recipes and stories turned out to be such a big hit that Ford eventually started printing spin-off cookbooks like *Favorite Recipes from Famous Eating Places.*

Over the years, a number of Kentucky eateries

nations of the original dining room, Kilbern's is keeping alive the legacy of grand hotel cuisine with a lineup of Kentucky Proud items and a new menu featuring regionally inspired dishes named after famous Lexingtonians.

To see what the locals are eating, pop in at lunchtime and sample the very popular buffet, which includes a salad bar and desserts such as Kilbern's original bread pudding. Unpretentious as it is satisfying, the fare can include corn bread fried flat as pancakes, creamy corn pudding, oven-fried potatoes, baked chicken and falling-apart pot roast with large chunks of celery and carrots.

With its starched linens and chandeliers seemingly in time-capsule condition, the dining room is both inviting and nostalgic. The waitresses are friendly and if you're lucky, you might get one of them to talk about the hotel ghosts or the hidden tunnels in the building, a remnant from its Cold War days as a civil defense bomb shelter. Relive the glory days of classic American hotel dining at the Campbell House and see for yourself why Kilbern's is a Fabulous Food Find.

were featured on the illustrated pages of this volume and although many of them have long since closed their doors, landmarks such as Harrodsburg's Beaumont Inn, Berea's Boone Tavern and the Old Talbott Tavern in Bardstown are still going strong. Another is Kilbern's, the restaurant at Lexington's Campbell House, and a local institution since the early 1950s.

Tony Adams grew up in the area and remembers the faux-colonial hotel in its heyday, when high rollers and card sharks used to come in and make a night of it in the lounge and restaurant. Little did he know that he'd return one day and take the helm of the hotel kitchen as its executive chef. Although the Campbell House has joined the Crowne Plaza chain and despite several reincar-

Kirchhoff's Bakery

118 Market House Square
Paducah, Kentucky 42001
(270) 442-7117

59

Nestled on the banks of the Ohio, Paducah is typical of the many historic river towns that dot the state. The Market House Square district has changed little since the late 1800s, and Kirchhoff's Bakery, the oldest bakery in town, still occupies the same site it did when it opened in 1873.

Kirchhoff's began at the hands of Franz and Hannah Kirchhoff, German immigrants who got their start selling groceries and baked goods from the banks of the Ohio River. They soon opened a small bakery and relied on Old World tradition and European baking techniques to produce specialties that made Kirchhoff's a household name in the region.

By the 1920s, the small bakeshop had become one of the largest bakeries in the state.

Unfortunately, a disastrous fire in the 1950s ended the family's involvement in the business, but after years of neglect, talk turned to the reestablishment of a bakery in the same location. In 1996, descendants of the Kirchhoffs decided to buy the property back from the city and reopen. Great-great-great granddaughter Ginny Kirchhoff, a graduate of the Professional Baker Program at Sullivan University, proved to be the ideal candidate to oversee the venture.

Today, the Kirchhoff's handiwork is on display in a wide assortment of bakery items including dozens of cookies and bars and more than three dozen breads and rolls.

The breads can be enjoyed by themselves at home or in a number of delicious deli sandwiches made fresh on the spot. Favorites include the old-fashioned BLT, the smoked pork loin on sourdough topped with coleslaw, deep-fried oysters on a house bun with pickle and remoulade, Saint Andre brie with bacon and tomato, and the Kirchhoff club with turkey, smoked ham, bacon and Cheddar. Don't miss the pimento cheese and bacon sandwich, a tangy, grilled treat with homemade pimento cheese, crisp bacon and thin slices of red onion on sourdough or rye. Because Ginny Kirchhoff is keeping her family tradition alive, this downtown bakery is one of Kentucky's Fabulous Food Finds.

Knoth's Bar-B-Q

728 US Highway 62
Grand Rivers, Kentucky 42045
(270) 362-8580

60

When you find yourself in western Kentucky, near the twin lakes of Kentucky Lake and Lake Barkley, be sure to stop at Knoth's Bar-B-Q in Grand Rivers. Knoth's, which rhymes with "oaths," is a fairly large restaurant with a lot of seating, compared to most pit joints. But as with your typical barbecue place, the menu here is very basic and consists of several types of pit-cooked meats, in addition to burgers, simple sandwiches and fries. But most people go there for the 'cue, so why bother with anything else? One of the most popular orders at this straightforward roadside eatery is the pulled pork plate with cole slaw, French fries, and bread, which comes to less than $10.00 with a soft drink and tax.

For many, the pork at Knoth's counts as

Like the sauce at Knoth's? Take a bottle home with you.

Ed McMahon made the 'cue at Knoth's famous in 1969. Call before you come, though; they close for the winter.

the gold standard for Kentucky barbecue. Despite the 14 hours of smoking they get, the meaty shoulders are never overcooked and have just the right amount of natural juice and sweetness. Mounded on a soft bun with a slathering of sweet, mustardy sauce, a pork sandwich makes the perfect to-go item. Hugh Knoth, the owner, is usually in the kitchen and he often stops by to check on his guests himself. His parents opened the restaurant in 1966, right about the time work on nearby Barkley Dam wrapped up, and just three years later, they got their big break when sidekick Ed McMahon told *Tonight Show* host Johnny Carson that he had eaten some wonderful barbecue at Knoth's. "Dad always said that's what broke us open for business," says Hugh Knoth. Ed McMahon wasn't the only one who thought Knoth's was the place to go for good western Kentucky barbecue, though, and that's what makes it one of my Fabulous Food Finds.

Kurtz Restaurant

418 East Stephen Foster Avenue
Bardstown, Kentucky 40004
(502) 348-8964

61

Located across the street from My Old Kentucky Home in an inviting stone cottage, Kurtz's has been serving up good Bluegrass cooking in Bardstown for over 70 years — so that must mean they know what they're doing. "Originally our family started this restaurant in 1937 serving meals from our home," says Mary Kurtz Dick. "This was long before fast food restaurants, country clubs and drive-ins." Over the years, this has became a place to gather and dine, and on any given night a wide variety of customers — some locals, some out-of-towners — come together for signature items like roast turkey breast with homemade dressing, potatoes and gravy and scrumptious biscuit pudding with bourbon sauce. By the end of the evening, it seems that everybody knows everybody else, that is, if they didn't know them already before coming in.

Got a sweet tooth? Check out the pie safe at Kurtz's in Bardstown, the Bourbon Capital of the World.

Turkey and gravy is a year-round favorite at
Kurtz Restaurant.

At Kurtz Restaurant three generations serve up American diner standards such as hot beef sandwiches and traditional southern dishes like skillet-fried chicken with mashed potatoes and milk gravy that have earned them favorable write ups in publications such as *The New York Times* and *Southern Living*. The skillet fried corn bread — moist and fluffy on the inside and crispy on the outside, thanks to a bit of bacon grease — is considered by many to be the best in the state.

Other popular items at Kurtz's include Virginia and country ham, both served with baked apples and potatoes. And since the fried chicken is so good that people drive all the way from Cincinnati for it, it makes appearances in other dinners that combine it with fried country ham and chicken livers. Dessert, however, is what makes the place special for many. An old-fashioned pie safe holds an enticing selection of pies — usually coconut, chocolate and lemon — all with two-inch high, golden meringues that make them hard to resist. Beautiful pies in a beautiful pie safe — this view is just one of the things that make Kurtz Restaurant one of Kentucky's 111 Fabulous Food Finds.

Le Deauville

199 North Limestone Road
Lexington, Kentucky 40507
(859) 246-0999

62

For a real taste of France in the Bluegrass, visit the distinctive red brick building with the elegant bank of green French doors across from the campus of Transylvania University. Perched stylishly on a corner, the inviting bistro — one of the best French restaurants to hit the Kentucky dining scene in a long while — might be more at home on the streets of Paris or in a cobblestone lane of a Normandy village than in the middle of Kentucky thoroughbred country. The art-nouveau advertising boards touting beer, wine and espresso in French only add to the allure. Named

*Endive with bleu cheese – a classic
touch on your French bistro experience.*

for Lexington's French sister city of Deauville, a charming beachside city in Normandy known for its stud farms and racetracks, Le Deauville has managed to cook up some of the region's very best French food.

Inside the inviting building, slowly twirling fans on high tin ceilings and graceful tiled floors add to the impression that one has been transported to a genuine café in the heart of Europe. Cozy banquettes and tables covered in white linen, dark wainscoting and French artwork on the walls complete the illusion. Occasional French accents in the background lend an extra bit of authenticity. The overall feel of the eatery is casual yet slightly upscale, and the service is friendly and attentive without coming across as overbearing. It's a good backdrop for a quick bite or leisurely dinner of enjoyable continental standards such as roasted rack of lamb with ratatouille and mint bordelaise, duck a l'orange with oyster mushrooms or hanger steak with gratin potatoes. There are also classic entrées such as osso bucco and bouillabaisse, and for starters you'll discover onion soup gratinée, escargot in garlic butter, goat cheese salad and endive with bleu cheese. And to end your experience at Le Deauville, there is always a wonderful selection of artisan cheeses as well as traditional French favorites such as crème brûlée and apple tart.

It's also the place to come for one of my favorites, steamed mussels with French fries, and you can get them prepared five different ways here. You can get them steamed with Pernod, Polynesian curry, or spicy tomato or you can have them with white wine, garlic and bacon or with lemon grass and coconut milk. There's even a Tuesday night special that gets you all the mussels and fries you can eat for $16.50. On Monday nights you can eat all the crepes you want for $19.50. Well-prepared classic bistro favorites in a restaurant named for Kentucky's horse-loving sister city in France — is it any wonder why I think Le Deauville is one of the most Fabulous Food Finds in Kentucky? Give their French fare a try and you'll agree.

Lynn's Paradise Café

984 Barret Avenue
Louisville, Kentucky 40204
(502) 583-3447

63

Pan-fried pecan chicken in Woodford Reserve mustard maple cream sauce. Gingersnap encrusted cod with homemade guava ketchup. Hoppin' Juan, a black bean chili piled high with organic jasmine rice, zesty tropical

Lynn Winter's tasty version of the hot brown.

mango chile salsa, cheddar cheese, sour cream and cumin scented blue corn tortillas. The food at Lynn's Paradise Café is as colorful and eclectic as its owner. Lynn Winter, a former woodworker, sold her tools and opened Lynn's Paradise Café in 1991, intent on creating a unique setting to attract a diverse group of people from around the world. Today, her funky diner with its cultivated kitsch in the Highlands neighborhood of Louisville has gained cult status among foodies across the Bluegrass and beyond. Among the many accolades Winter has received, *Bon Appetit* named Lynn's Paradise Café one of the 100 best neighborhood restaurants in the United States and *Esquire* proclaimed it one of the most fun.

To say the least, Lynn's quirky diner features hometown cooking with a twist, be it the signature bourbon ball French toast for breakfast, the bleu grass burger, a half-pound patty of Kentucky grass-fed beef with handmade organic cheeses, for lunch or the Cajun-spiced fried catfish with a mustard shallot sauce at dinner. Inside, diners discover — among other things — a whitewashed tree that rises through the ceiling and previous winners of the Ugly Lamp Contest, which Winter started at the Kentucky State Fair in 1999. The place is homey and surreal at the same time, but the unusual atmosphere begins long before you get to the door. Outside, colorfully painted offbeat concrete statuary greets hungry guests, and a fountain in the shape of a giant coffeepot splashes happily away. This quirky outlook on life makes Lynn's Paradise Café one of the state's most unusual Fabulous Food Finds.

Magee's Bakery

8188 Orangeburg Road
Maysville, Kentucky 41056
(606) 759-4882

In Mason County a sweet delicacy has entrenched itself as part of the food folklore in Kentucky – and Maggee's Bakery is its home. A simple confection made from milk, eggs, sugar and butter, it's known as transparent pie or transparent pudding and its origins go back to frontier days when families would make desserts from the ingredients left on hand when no fruits or nuts were available. An added plus was the fact that it required no refrigeration and it would go on to serve as the basis for pecan and chess pie. If you like sugary custard and flaky crust, transparent pie is for you.

Back in 1941, when Ruth and Leslie Magee opened a shop specializing in fruit pies, cakes and other baked goods, they immediately recognized the demand for this local favorite and decided to keep the tradition

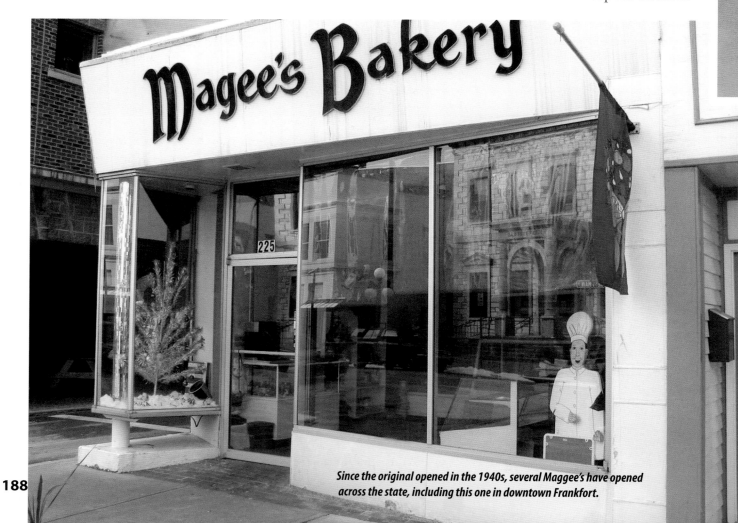

Since the original opened in the 1940s, several Maggee's have opened across the state, including this one in downtown Frankfort.

Transparent Pie
$ 7.00

Magee's BAKERY
759-4882

alive. Today Maggee's transparent pies and puddings are still popular items — although they call them window pies or clear pies in other parts — and Maysville has become the epicenter for the transparent pie market, with numerous orders shipped throughout the United States every year. Judy and Ronald Dickson purchased the bakery in 1972, and since then they have mailed tarts, also known as puddings, and pies all over the world. They relocated the bakery from its downtown location and today it sits off a windy road outside of Maysville. It's worth the drive, though. Take a bite of transparent pie and you'll see why Maggee's Bakery is one of the Fabulous Food Finds in Kentucky.

Maker's Mark Bourbon House & Lounge

446 South Fourth Street
Louisville, Kentucky 40202
(502) 568-9009

65

When the Fourth Street Live entertainment district had its grand opening in October 2004, the Maker's Mark Bourbon House & Lounge was one of the first businesses to participate in the revitalization of downtown Louisville. An impressive 57-foot long wooden bar outlined in marble, chic furnishings and customized art-glass fixtures hinted at good things to come. Today, this upscale eatery is still going strong and it attracts a faithful clientele of locals and out-of-towners alike. It's also a popular stop along the Urban Bourbon Trail, a collection of Louisville establishments that promote the state's rich distilling heritage while serving Kentucky whiskey and bourbon-based products.

In addition to numerous cocktails and more than 60 bourbons available at the bar, guests can sample a wide variety of dishes from seasonal menus that make the most of local products. Appetizer selections might include items such as the canapé Lucile with homemade lamb sausage, Munster cheese, micro greens and Dijon bourbon mustard, or the rock

shrimp popcorn, shrimp that is marinated in bourbon buttermilk, deep fried, and served with bourbon mustard aioli and sweet chili sauce.

For main courses, diners could find dishes such as grilled Colorado lamb with Parisian herbed potatoes and bourbon mint demi; Tanglewood free range chicken with asparagus tips, sherry-glazed pearl onions and sweet potato purée infused with bourbon and thyme; prime beef filet with morel mushroom demi glace, bourbon creamed sweet corn, thyme and fried okra; or veal medallions with cognac persillade, artichoke bottom stuffed with spinach and potato, and bourbon and chili glazed carrots. Sweets such as the signature bourbon balls or the turf lawn torte — a concoction of bourbon, figs, pecan and chocolate — make the perfect end to a leisurely meal or a quick bite at Maker's Mark Lounge. Sleek and stylish, Maker's Mark Lounge is one of Kentucky's newest Fabulous Food Finds. Sample the bourbon-themed fare in the heart of downtown Derby City and find out why.

Marshall's Backstretch Diner

232 West Main Street
Frankfort, Kentucky 40601
(502) 223-5006

66

If you've seen the 2006 movie *Dreamer*, the moving tale about a trainer and his daughter who rehabilitate a badly injured horse to run in the Breeder's Cup, you've seen some of the best scenery the Bluegrass has to offer. Set entirely in Kentucky, it gave movie-goers all over the world an inside look at the industry that has made the state famous. In addition to tree-lined country lanes, stone fences, stables and magnificent horse farms, it also provided glimpses into a local eatery or two. One of them was a decades-long favorite in downtown Frankfort, Marshall's Diner, which was portrayed as the Backstretch Diner in the movie. After writer and director John Gatins and his crew left town, however, it was renamed Marshall's Backstretch Diner. The name might have changed, but the good news is that the no-nonsense approach to affordable diner fare hasn't, and today's proprietors Della and Elbert Bowman offer the same good food at the same good prices.

Popular items at this old-fashioned diner include country-fried steak (top) and the Backstretch burger (bottom).

This earns them a spot as a Fabulous Food Find.

Like most diners across the country, the Backstretch has a menu with typical breakfast selections in the morning and a variety of sandwiches and plate meals available during the rest of the day. Said to be the best burger in Frankfort by many, the Backstretch signature item is the Backstretch burger, which has six ounces of lean ground beef cooked to order and topped with melted cheese, grilled onions and mushrooms.

Aside from burgers and dogs, hot sandwiches include country fried steak, pulled pork, breaded cod, hamburger steak, chuck wagons, sloppy joes and tuna melts. Cold sandwiches include pimento cheese, BLT, bologna, roast beef, country ham and chicken salad. Lunch and dinner platters include pork tenderloin, country fried steak, hot roast beef, country ham and fried shrimp.

Merrick Inn

1074 Merrick Drive
Lexington, Kentucky 40502
(859) 269-5417

It's no secret that many consider Kentucky to be holy ground for connoisseurs of fried chicken. So, if residents of the Bluegrass consistently favor a restaurant's fried bird, chances are it must be awfully good. Considered a bastion for the most discerning fried chicken lovers since the 1970s, Lexington's Merrick Inn is without a doubt at the top of the long list of Kentucky restaurants serving up the state's most famous dish. With its delicate balance of spices and crispy coating that preserves the moistness of the meat inside, the fried chicken at Merrick Inn puts a whole new spin on the phrase finger-licking good.

The main dining room of the manor house of Merrick Place – for many years one of the finest thoroughbred farms in the Bluegrass Region – is often filled to capacity and buzzes with lively conversation. The owners, the Murrays, pride themselves on their immaculate upkeep of the elegant restaurant and visitors enjoy superb southern cuisine and innovative American dishes, complemented by attentive service.

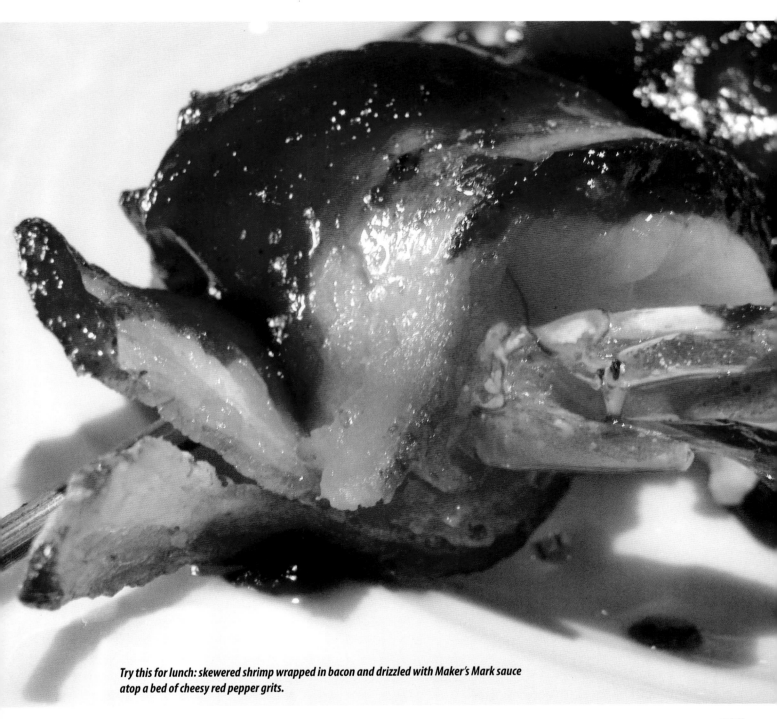

Try this for lunch: skewered shrimp wrapped in bacon and drizzled with Maker's Mark sauce atop a bed of cheesy red pepper grits.

Although the fried chicken has made them famous, a sizeable number of other items make Merrick Inn a popular destination for any respectable gourmand of Bluegrass cuisine. Much sought-after appetizers include fried banana peppers — not as spicy as anticipated and with a light, crispy breading and flavorful seasonings — and Maker's Mark shrimp, which are wrapped in bacon and served over roasted red pepper cheese grits. A wonderful salad to start with is the green goddess, a classic mix of iceberg and romaine lettuce with fresh egg and applewood bacon.

But if chicken's not your thing, try the walleye pike, an 8-ounce filet fried crispy and served with homemade tartar sauce. An assortment of steaks and chops can be had as well, and a hit with the locals is the pecan-crusted pork tenderloin topped with a spoonful of bourbon apple chutney. Merrick Inn has an extensive wine list, and cocktails can be enjoyed in the lounge before or after dinner. Weather permitting, lighter fare and entertainment are offered on the weekends on the patio, one of the most attractive and comfortable in the area. Wherever you sit, give the fried chicken a try and see why Merrick Inn is one of my Fabulous Food Finds.

Old paintings found in the attic add a bit of interest to this ceiling.

Miguel's Pizza

1890 Natural Bridge Road
Slade, Kentucky 40376
(606) 663-1975

68

Tucked away in a clearing on a bend of the road in Natural Bridge State Resort Park sits a small yet eye-catching wooden building with a bright coat of lemon yellow paint. Make the trip there and you'll not only get to see some wonderful natural scenery along the way, you'll most likely taste some of the best pizza you've had in a long while. Although rock climbers and hikers have known about it for years, Miguel's Pizza is a great stop whether or not you've got chalk on your hands or a pack on your back.

Miguel's has an extensive selection of pizza toppings that range from standards such as pepperoni and sausage to more obscure items such as feta cheese and even pasta, potatoes, and rice. Whether

getting a whole pie or a couple of slices, guests pick up an order sheet at the counter and mark their preferences before sitting down at one of the old school bus seats scattered about. Sandwiches and calzones are available as well, and you can also get ice cream and sodas, including Ale 8-One, the local ginger ale. For those wanting to do a bit of shopping, Miguel's Pizza sells a variety of apparel with their logo, in addition to climbing gear. Not only that, free wireless is available and climbers can pay $2 per night to pitch a tent out back. Although the setting is somewhat remote, a steady stream of nature lovers from far and away ensures that Miguel's Pizza has a cosmopolitan feel. A good setting and good pizza make Miguel's Pizza one of our Fabulous Food Finds.

Mike Linnig's

There aren't too many places in Kentucky, or in the country for that matter, quite like Mike Linnig's. Some nights it bustles with activity and lively conversation, others — especially on sultry summer evenings — flickering lanterns cast a mellow mood over the picnic area under a canopy of towering oak trees. But whatever the atmosphere, the seafood is always a hit with the customers, and since 1925 fish lovers have been flocking to this southwest Louisville restaurant for generous, yet affordable, portions of seafood and home cooking.

They close down for two months over the winter, so check before you make the trek to Mike Linnig's for huge fish sandwiches and more.

Linnig's restaurant sits near the banks of the Ohio River, on land that was a working family farm when Mike Linnig and his wife opened a small roadside stall selling fresh fruit and vegetables in the early 1900s. People called the stand "Mike's Place" and eventually it grew into a little eatery serving freshly squeezed apple cider, cold sandwiches and candies. Fried fish sandwiches soon joined the menu, and the same basic preparation is still in use today.

This winning recipe has resulted in readers of the *Courier-Journal* voting Mike Linnig's the best fish sandwich in the region on more than one occasion. One bite and the reason becomes clear: Mike Linning's sandwich is the largest and tastiest in town, with gigantic pieces of whitefish coated in a tender, crunchy batter that stands up nicely to the house-made tartar sauce studded with chopped sweet pickle. But there's much more than fried fish and hushpuppies on the menu. Fried clams, crawfish, oyster stew, peel-and-eat shrimp, clam chowder, turtle soup, frog legs, pan-fried oysters, battered salmon and crab cakes are just some of the seafood items available, and for the landlubbers there are chicken, onion rings, burgers, pork cutlets, rib-eye sandwiches, steaks and more.

Already in its third generation of family operation, Mike Linning's survived the flood of 1937 and a disastrous fire in 1966 that destroyed the original building. It is sure to be a culinary icon for many more generations to come, and this is why Mike Linning's counts as one of the Fabulous Food Finds in Kentucky.

Miller House

301 East Fifth Street
Owensboro, Kentucky 42303
(270) 685-5878

70

In Owensboro, dinner guests can sit down for a homey meal in what used to be one of the city's finest mansions. "We want people to feel like they're in a house, not a restaurant," says Jeanne Kirk, who along with her husband, Larry, opened the Miller House in the spring of 2009 after two years of painstaking renovation and restoration. Built in 1905 for coal baron Elmer Miller and his wife, Lizzy, the house was touted as a "model of beauty, elegance and convenience" shortly after its construction and had fallen on hard times until the Kirks found it. But according to Larry, it's almost as they envisioned it today. Comforting hues of muted colors adorn the walls and quarter-sawn parquet floors trimmed with Brazilian cherry gleam throughout the elegant residence, which offers seating on three levels.

The Kirks describe the fare at the Miller House as "American cooking with a southern drawl," and items such as fried green tomatoes with red pepper coulis, shrimp and grits, chicken and country ham, and fried catfish with roasted corn remoulade bear this out.

Kasey Kirk-Dillow, their daughter and Sullivan University graduate, heads up the kitchen at the restaurant, and her signature dishes include crab cakes served with roast potatoes and ratatouille, and meatloaf with demi-glace, mashed potatoes and sautéed green beans. The dessert selection changes daily, but a regular feature is the molasses pie, a sweet concoction baked from an old recipe passed down from the first lady of the house, Lizzy Miller. The fried green tomatoes are a big draw and the Kirks did a good deed in saving an old house — that's why I think their restaurant is one of many Fabulous Food Finds in western Kentucky.

Moonlite Bar-B-Q Inn

2840 West Parrish Avenue
Owensboro, Kentucky 42301
(270) 684-8143

When you're in Owensboro, the unmistakable smell of smoky meat usually lingers in the air. Follow your nose and you'll probably end up at Moonlite Bar-B-Q Inn, a western Kentucky institution since 1963. Started by Catherine and Pappy Bosley, who made it into a success despite their lack of restaurant experience, Moonlite Bar-B-Q is consistently rated one of the top barbecue destinations in the country today. It receives regular coverage from the national media, and one of the things that has made them famous is the all-you-can-eat buffet.

Ask most anyone in Owensboro about the buffet at Moonlite Bar-B-Q, and they will tell you it is spectacular. It occupies its own room, with meats and vegetables on one half, and salads and desserts on the other. On the meat side you'll find pulled pork, chicken, ribs and slices of meaty, salty coun-

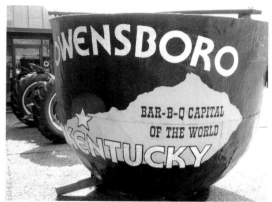

try ham that fit perfectly into their buttery dinner rolls. There's also beef brisket with a butter-soft interior and chewy crust of black that comes from hours in the pit and mutton, tender as pot roast and available two ways: chopped or pulled. The meats are generally unsauced, and back at the table diners can choose what sauce, if any, they want for seasoning. The "mutton dip" is an unctuous blend used to baste the meat as it smokes, and the other is a rich orange emulsion with the slight tang of tomato and vinegar. In addition, bottles of "Very Hot Sauce" can be had for those who need a bit of heat.

With its impressive array of house-made salads, old-fashioned sides and home-style vegetables, the Moonlite buffet evens attracts a fair share of vegetarians to its steaming pans of macaroni and cheese, mashed potatoes drizzled with butter, green beans, creamed corn, braised cabbage, and cheesy broccoli casserole, just to name a few. The dessert selection is huge as well and includes peanut butter pie, carrot cake, chocolate pie, pecan pie, cheese cake, lemon icebox pie and cherry cobbler, most of which can be purchased whole at the front counter and taken home if there's no room for sweets at the end of the buffet. With all this good food, do you have to ask why the Moonlite is one of Kentucky's Fabulous Food Finds?

My Old Kentucky Dinner Train

602 North Third Street
Bardstown, Kentucky 40004
(502) 348-7300

72

Photo by Benny Gettinger

I t's a shame that train travel is a thing of the past in most parts of the country today. Every once in a while, though, you'll find something that reminds us of the glory days of the railroad. A restored depot. A historic trestle. My Old Kentucky Dinner Train in Bardstown, Kentucky. The R.J. Corman Railroad Company has run this one-of-a-kind attraction since 1988, over the years showing numerous visitors a whole new meaning to the idea of meals on wheels. Considering the relaxing ride and beautiful scenery that come with your meal, it's hardly surprising that this is one of Kentucky's most unique and popular food finds.

Photo by Benny Gettinger

209

Traditional desserts like apple dumplings are a sweet end to this moveable feast.

Photo by R.J. Corman

Operating year-round on different schedules, My Old Kentucky Dinner Train features three beautifully restored dining cars from the 1940s with elegant interiors where traditional tables of four provide space that's intimate enough for private conversation, yet open enough to chat with your neighbors. During the trip of two and half hours, the train meanders past the historic Sisters of Charity Motherhouse and through beautiful countryside on Jim Beam property and in the Bernheim Forest as the executive chef prepares a delicious meal.

For lunch, guests enjoy a three-course special that begins with the signature "golden spike" salad of mixed greens, candied pecans, golden raisins, cherry tomatoes and bleu cheese crumbles and then move on to an entrée choice that includes bourbon-braised prime rib over garlic mashed potatoes and roasted carrots. For dinner, a starter of Kentucky beer cheese is served before the salad, and main courses include bourbon barrel smoked pork tenderloin and roasted bourbon chicken with vegetables. For dessert, guests can choose the daily cobbler with whipped cream, Kern's Derby Pie or a warm apple dumpling with cinnamon sauce. My Old Kentucky Dinner Train is a moveable feast, to say the least, and that's why it's one of my 111 Fabulous Food Finds.

The Oakroom

500 South Fourth Street
Louisville, Kentucky 40204
(502) 585-3200

In the 1990s gourmands in the Bluegrass were thrilled to learn the Oakroom at the Seelbach Hotel had added another sprig of laurel to its culinary wreath by receiving the coveted Five Diamond Award from AAA. Today, Kentucky's first and only five-diamond restaurant, one of a very select number in the country, continues a tradition of elegance and fine dining that make the Oakroom a must for food lovers across the state.

If for nothing else, this Louisville icon earns five stars for its lavish décor. What was once a turn-of-the-century billiards room for gentlemen received a stunning makeover by renowned designer Marie Bordelon and now the intricately carved oak throughout the room gleams. Set off with customized textiles and luxurious fabrics, it's not surprising that the Oakroom wins regular accolades ranking it among "America's 50

Photos courtesy of the Seelbach Hilton

Best Hotel Restaurants" by *Food and Wine* magazine and "Our Favorite Romantic Restaurants" by *Southern Living* magazine.

Then there's the history. Among the many notables hosted there since construction in 1905 were F. Scott Fitzgerald, who received inspiration to write *The Great Gatsby* while staying at the Seelbach, and none other than Al Capone himself, who had his own private dining area outfitted with special mirrors and secret panels to facilitate getaways during police raids. Today dinner guests can reserve the Blackjack Room and enjoy a meal where the most infamous gangster of the 1920s sat.

As would be expected of a five-diamond restaurant, the carefully crafted cuisine at the Oakroom sets the bar for fine dining in the region. Oakroom chefs support local farmers and artisans, cultivating a "New American" approach to food preparation with menus featuring seasonal produce. In the past, selections have included items such as Vidalia onion bisque with Gruyère grilled cheese, chives, and Benton's bacon and Kentucky bison strip served alongside brown butter gnocchi and white chocolate cauliflower purée. No matter what you order, the Oakroom will provide an unforgettable dinner experience, proving it's one of the region's most Fabulous Food Finds of all.

Old Hickory Pit Bar-B-Q

338 Washington Avenue
Owensboro, Kentucky 42301
(270) 926-9000

Owensboro is a town known for its barbecue, so it's not surprising that it has a number of joints that receive regular praise from food gurus across the nation. But when you're in Owensboro and ask the natives what the very best place for 'cue is, chances are they'll tell you to go to the Old Hickory Bar-B-Q. One reason why it's so good is the smoky flavor that laces its slow-cooked meats, a characteristic that draws on five generations of pit master tradition.

Although the Old Hickory name was officially coined in 1954, the culinary roots of this western Kentucky landmark go back to 1918, when blacksmith Charles "Pappy" Foreman began roasting mutton on a pit near Frederica Street. The mutton, rich, moist and ever so slightly redolent of musk, is still a specialty more than 90 years later. Pork, turkey, beef, chicken and ham were eventually added to the lineup, and the Foreman clan soon came to be known for their skills at the pit. Today, guests at Old Hickory can enjoy these barbecued

meats in sandwich form or on a plate with bread, pickles, onion and a choice of two sides such as French fries, onion rings, barbecued beans, cole slaw and potato salad. Burgers and catfish are also on the menu, and many consider the thick, slow-cooked burgoo the best in the state. A variety of desserts are available as well, but the pecan pie and lemon icebox pie have gained a loyal following among the barbecue fans with a sweet tooth. Try the barbecue at Old Hickory and see why I think it deserves to be one of the 111 Fabulous Food Finds in Kentucky.

Old Hickory Bar-B-Q

"SIX GENERATIONS OF QUALITY BAR-B-Q"

Mutton			
Hind Qtr (Ham)	9.79/LB	Turkey Breast	7.25/LB
ore Qtr (Shoulder)	9.25/LB	Beef (Sliced)	9.25/LB
oin	7.95/LB	Chicken (Whole)	3.79/LB
Mutton Ribs	6.95/LB	Chicken (Half)	3.79/LB
Chopped Mutton	5.95/LB	Potato Salad	2.90/PT
		Cole Slaw	2.90/PT
Pork		Bar-B-Q Beans	2.90/PT
Pork (Sliced)	9.79/LB	Burgoo	3.00/PT
Pork Ribs	9.50/LB	Burgoo	4.75/QT
Chopped Pork	5.95/LB	Burgoo	13.25/GAL
		Chili	3.25/PT
Bar-B-Q Ham	7.25/LB	Bean Soup	2.75/PT

Old Stone Inn

6905 Shelbyville Road
Simpsonville, Kentucky 40067
(502) 722-8200

ompleted in the very early 1800s as a family dwelling, the Old Stone Inn counts as one of the oldest eating establishments in the Commonwealth. Aside from its status as a recognized local landmark, the rustic structure is listed on the National Register of Historic Places as well. Over the centuries, it has served as a stagecoach stop, tavern, residence, inn and, since the 1920s, a restaurant, and today there aren't many people in Jefferson County who haven't heard of the Old Stone Inn.

Allen and Robert Purnell purchased the restaurant in 1987 and today's proprietor is Shelley Thompson; the chef is Jerrett Berry. Although trendy dishes such a crispy calamari with lemon basil aioli and red clam sauce and encrusted goat cheese salad have made their way to the menu, traditional Bluegrass influences are clearly visible in popular dishes such as the southern fried chicken and country ham, both served with greens, mashed potatoes and gravy. Other sought-after items are the shrimp and grits, steak and fries, and the bourbon barrel pork chop, a 14-ounce Porterhouse cut that is smoked, grilled and then served with grits and seasonal

vegetables. Popular as well are the hot brown and the catfish with slaw and fries. For a great starter, begin with the fried, cornmeal-crusted green tomatoes with goat cheese, baby spinach, crispy country ham and spicy remoulade. Like the rest of the menu, dessert selections change seasonally, but guests with a sweet tooth can usually count on items such as bread pudding with bourbon sauce, lemon berry chiffon cake, and bourbon pecan pie. Good Kentucky cooking and over two centuries of history make the Old Stone Inn one of my favorite Fabulous Food Finds.

A slice of fried green tomato and crisp bacon make the Southern burger a hit at Shelley Thompson's restaurant.

The Old Talbott Tavern

107 West Stephen Foster Avenue
Bardstown, Kentucky 40004
(502) 348-3494

Since the late 1700s, travelers to Bardstown have received shelter, food and drink at the Old Talbott Tavern, one of the oldest stagecoach stops in America. Although they arrive in automobiles today, and not by horse and carriage like they used to, the same sense of welcome remains. When visitors walk into the Old Talbott Tavern, creaking floorboards recall years of hospitality, and it's easy to imagine the pub bustling with guests downing an ale or a hearty supper before an early departure the next morning.

In the dining room fried chicken, country ham, and hot browns are popular items on the menu, as are slow-cooked pot roast and cornmeal breaded catfish. House specialties include the Queen Marie salad with chicken, seasonal fruit, cottage cheese and a hand-dipped corn fritter, and the chicken Phillipe, boneless breast braised in a tangy burgundy sauce served over wild rice and sautéed mushrooms. To start their meal, patrons can choose items like slow-simmer burgoo, stuffed button mushroom and stagecoach fries, crispy fried potatoes topped with bacon and melting cheese. For a twist on a classic, try the green tomatoes, which are fried in beer batter and topped with Parmesan cheese and red and green peppers. For dessert, chess pie and homemade fruit cobblers are still some of the favorites.

The Kentucky hot brown at the Old Talbott

Peppery milk gravy covers the country-fried steak at Bardstown's Old Talbott Tavern.

The Old Talbott also has a Bourbon Bar that offers light snacks, drinks and live entertainment on the weekends, and visitors will find souvenirs, Kentucky cookbooks and other interesting items in the gift shop. In addition, travelers seeking lodging while in Bardstown, will find five rooms available at in the Old Talbott Tavern, all decorated with period antiques. Because you don't find too many places like the Old Talbott Tavern anymore, it's one of my Fabulous Food Finds in Kentucky.

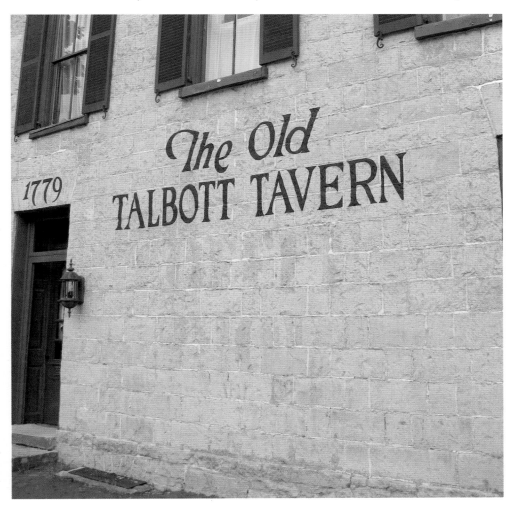

Ollie's Trolley

978 South Third Street
Louisville, Kentucky 40208
(502) 583-5214

77

You don't need a ticket to hop on this trolley. Once part of a national chain in the 1970s, the original still survives in Old Louisville.

In Old Louisville, at the corner of Third and Kentucky, stands something of a fast-food relic. It's Ollie's Trolley, a vestige of the days when the Ollie's Trolley chain had outlets across the country — not to mention a dozen scattered throughout Louisville, its city of inception. In addition to walk-in buildings shaped like bright red-and-yellow street cars, the chain's gimmick featured a secret blend of 23 herbs and spices — more than twice as many as the Colonel used in his fried chicken — and a legendary owner, a fastidious coot by the name of Ollie, who insisted that his burgers be served rare and only with his special secret sauce. The sauce, incidentally, is a slightly spicy mayonnaise-based concoction with herbs somewhat akin to Thousand Island dressing.

The Ollie Burger "with everything" has a thick, flavorful third-pound patty on a bun, topped with a slice of melted mozzarella cheese and dressed with a thick slice of fresh tomato, crisp lettuce, sliced raw white onion and a slathering of "secret" sauce. The menu offers several alternatives to the Ollie, including a bacon burger and a chili burger, not to mention a chicken sandwich, fried fish, Polish sausage and fries tossed with black pepper and spices.

Like the Ollie's Trolleys of the good ol' days, this one is take-out only, but if you can't wait until you get home, there are a couple of metal tables in a corner of the tiny parking lot that circles where Ollie's is located. They only accept cash, but it's the last of a dying breed and that's why this little piece of fast-food history is one of my Fabulous Food Finds in Kentucky.

Parkette Drive In

1230 East New Circle Road
Lexington, Kentucky 40505
(859) 254-8723

78

When Lexington's landmark Parkette Drive In abruptly closed in 2003, residents feared a part of local history had been lost. And they said New Circle Road — a dirt lane when the Parkette first opened more than half a century before, out in what was considered the country — wouldn't look the same without the iconic green and red sign and the flashing neon lights that touted their famous chicken, fish and shrimp boxes. Fortunately for them, brothers Jeff Kaplan and Randy Kaplan — Philadelphia natives and nostalgia buffs who moved to Kentucky by way of Miami — were looking for a project. General contractors themselves, they got to work and did a lot of the hot, heavy work needed to get the Parkette Drive In up and running. Today Lexingtonians have their beloved drive in back — and its towering neon sign with the stylized carhop.

The sign, created shortly after the restaurant opened in the early 1950s, is over 30 feet tall and it costs $1,000 a year to replace the transformers and lights needed to maintain the sign. But this is just one of many touches the Kaplans have undertaken to preserve a slice of real Americana: the exterior of the building has been wrapped in the

quilted stainless steel typical of vintage diners and the black-and-white tiled interior sports a jukebox, pinball machines, and vinyl booths. A deck area at the back of the building is the ideal spot for visitors to congregate and enjoy the many antique roadsters and hobby cars that frequent the restaurant.

Food at Lexington's favorite drive in has remained largely unchanged, and the menu includes standard items such as shakes, malts, burgers, fries, onion rings and sandwiches. You can even get an order of tater tots, that seemingly dying breed of post-war convenience foods, which makes the perfect side in one of the popular "boxes" of fried chicken, fish and shrimp served with cole slaw and a roll. It's a rare holdover that has survived from the 50s, and that's why the Parkette Drive In is one of my Fabulous Food Finds.

Patti's 1880's Settlement

1759 J.H. O'Bryan Avenue
Grand Rivers, Kentucky 42045
(270) 362-8844

79

Who says you need to be a trained chef to run a good restaurant? "Chip, myself and even our mother never had a cooking lesson," says Michael Tullar, the owner of Patti's 1880's Settlement, a restaurant-turned-attraction in the small town of Grand Rivers, on the northern edge of the Land Between the Lakes. "We all love to eat and we've learned over the years what tastes good." This simple approach to food and cooking has gained them a faithful following and has won them many accolades, including official billing as the #1 Restaurant for Tourism by the Kentucky Department of Tourism.

What started out as a 20-seat ice cream parlor in 1977 took off after Tullar's mother, Patti, convinced his brother Chip to leave Los Angeles and take over the evening shift at the family restaurant. "My mother was the baker and daytime cook while Chip ran the place and was the evening cook," says Tullar. One of the first dishes created by Chip was a large pork chop that has become

The 2-inch pork chop is a signature item at Patti's.

a signature item at Patti's. Charbroiled and two inches thick, these chops garnered an award from the Kentucky Pork Producers Association and today they sell an average of 60,000 pounds per year. There's also a large array of steak, chicken, seafood, pasta, salad and sandwich items on the menu at Patti's, in addition to another specialty, the "mile high" meringue pies in lemon, chocolate and coconut.

Over the years, Patti's has grown to include various souvenir stores, gift shops and a café housed in reconstructed log cabins set among gardens, walkways and gazebos behind the main restaurant. It's a popular stop for tourists in search of a quick bite or an afternoon away from the campground. Some even come for the cooking lessons offered at Patti's nowadays. Charbroiled pork chops and meringue pies — give them a try and see why Patti's is one of the Fabulous Food Finds in Kentucky.

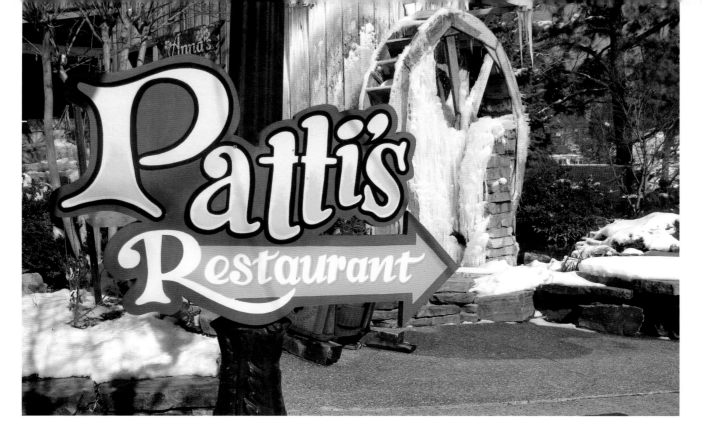

Peak Brothers

6353 US Highway 60 East
Waverly, Kentucky 42463
(270) 389-0267

When an early morning fire — the second in its history — destroyed a Union County culinary landmark on November 2, 2006, many feared that the end of an era had come. However, less than two years later, and just in time to celebrate its 60th anniversary, Peak Brothers Bar-B-Q rose from the ashes, much to the relief of barbecue fans across the country. The original version of the restaurant opened on the Fourth of July in 1948 when brothers Buddy and Barker Peak converted an old, boarded-up restaurant into a barbecue stand, and they soon had a steady stream of clientele flocking in. And this, despite the fact that neither of them knew the slightest thing about cooking.

"We hired a local janitor from one of the schools who knew how to run a pit," says Buddy. "He was supposed to stay a week or so, but he was here for more than 20 years. He was afraid we'd burn the meat." But, the Peak Brothers eventually became pit masters in their own right, and today Buddy's children carry on the legacy. Lady Bird Johnson thought the barbecue at Peak Brothers was so good that she sent them her regards in the 1960s; the original letter was salvaged from the

fire and still hangs on the wall today. Since Waverly is in the west, chopped mutton is a specialty here, and the Peaks serve it with a vinegary sauce with a lot of spice. In the barbecue department, country ham, beef, pork and chicken are available as well, however there is a variety of non-barbecue items ranging from "big mouth" sandwiches to steaks and fried chicken. A dozen appetizers, most of them fried, are available to start off the meal at Peak's, but be sure to try the beer battered pepper caps, Cheddar cheese balls or spicy fried dill pickles. Peak Brothers also opens for breakfast and the menu consists of their homemade pancakes, bacon and eggs, sausage, biscuits and good hot coffee. Breakfast or barbecue — the Peak Brothers have been doing it right for over six decades and that makes them one of the 111 Fabulous Food Finds in my book.

Porky Pig Diner

125 Park Boundary Road
Pig, Kentucky 42171
(270) 597-2422

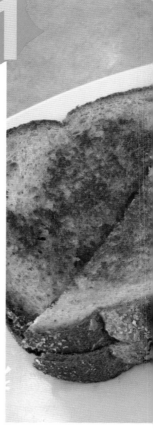

81

Unless you live in the immediate surroundings, a trip to Pig, Kentucky can require a bit of planning. The out-of-the-way community in Edmonson County is un-incorporated and to say that there's not much there except for a few buildings clustered near the intersection of KY 422 and KY 259 wouldn't be much of a stretch. One draw, however, is that it's just a few miles from world-famous Mammoth Cave so you might just find yourself in the vicinity some day on a road trip to Bowling Green. If you do – or even if you don't – make sure to stop in at the Porky Pig Diner and see why so many think it's a fabulous food find.

Housed in a tidy white building just steps from the junction, the Porky Pig Diner is typical of the many small, no-frills eateries that characterize the landscape of rural Kentucky: the interior is clean, the décor is minimal, the locals are friendly and the grub is down-to-earth and affordable. And at Porky Pig Diner, the food is excellent as well.

To find out what's on the menu, take a gander at the back wall and study the changeable letter sign where the selections run the gamut from standard breakfast fare to sandwiches and plate dinners. Although owners Calvin and Ramona make a mean patty melt and pork tenderloin sandwich, the two items that have evolved as the most popular are the home-smoked pit barbecue and the fried catfish. The barbecue is slow-cooked and smoky, and the catfish, served with crispy fries and hushpuppies, is perfectly seasoned and lightly breaded — give it a try and you'll understand how come so many say it's the best catfish they've ever had.

If you're looking for something different, head to Porky Pig Diner on a Sunday for the weekly breakfast buffet. In addition to all the standards, you'll find an old hard-to-find country favorite — biscuits with chocolate gravy. Whatever you get or whenever you go, make sure to stop and pet Pound Hound before you leave Porky Pig Diner. The stray basset hound just showed up a while back and today the droopy eyed pooch spends most of the day sleeping in front of the door and gets three meals a day — and a dish of ice cream at night — courtesy of Calvin and Ramona. Now that's one lucky dog — and Porky Pig Diner is a wonderful Food Find.

Proof on Main

702 West Main Street
Louisville, Kentucky 40202
(502) 217-6360

82

Even the most jaded of critics can't help but be impressed by the exciting blend of Kentucky artisanal foods, boutique American spirits and cutting edge décor that have come to characterize one of the most talked-about restaurants on the national dining scene. Part trendy bistro, part snazzy lounge, part contemporary art gallery, Proof on Main is the brainchild of restaurateur Drew Nieporent and local philanthropists Laura Lee Brown and Steve Wilson. Part of the 21c Museum Hotel on Louisville's old Distiller's Row, it opened in March 2006 and is a must see for anyone who enjoys good food and provocative art.

Avid collectors, Wilson and Brown dipped into their private stash to outfit the understated interior of the restaurant and hotel with a dazzling array of colorful

Red penguins and a breathing chandelier — hallmarks of a trip to the 21c Hotel.

Chickpea fritters with country ham have evolved as a signature starter at the ultra-trendy Proof on Main in downtown Louisville.

photographs, vibrant textiles, eye-catching sculptures and interactive displays. An outdoor chandelier – which *breathes* – by Austrian artist Werner Reiterer graces the entrance, and a life-size bronze satyr by San Francisco sculptor Larry Shank coyly greets new arrivals from its perch atop the bar. Nearby, some of Louisville's most recognized faces – the work of local artist Shayne Hull – gaze down from an exposed brick wall.

The 100-seat dining area next to the bar affords executive chef Michael Paley the opportunity to wow patrons with his own brand of culinary artistry while showing off modern American fare with Italian peasant leanings and flavors of the South. His passion for small family farms and locally grown produce is evident in the ever changing menu, which in the past has included Tuscan-inspired dishes such as Heritage Farms pork shank, buckwheat pappardelle with braised rabbit, bone-in bison tenderloin, and pork cheek milanese. Offerings like the Kentucky bison carpaccio with pickled wild ramps, the Weisenberger stone ground grits with Parmesan and the chickpea and country ham fritters highlight the flavors of the Bluegrass. Proof on Main is open for breakfast, lunch and dinner seven days a week, but the great art and great food make it one of my Fabulous Food Finds any time you go.

Ralph's Hickory Pit

739 North Green Street
Henderson, Kentucky 42420
(270) 826-5656

ood barbecue restaurants abound in Henderson, and Ralph's Hickory Pit has been a favorite with many since it opened in 1988. Aside from sandwiches, soups and burgers, the menu features a large assortment of barbecued items served sandwich-style or on platters with two sides, pickles, onion and bread. Choices include chicken, mutton, pork, ham, beef and smoked turkey. At Ralph's, the mutton, a regional staple, is slow-cooked until it's so moist and tender it resembles aged roast beef — something that makes the perfect match to the tangy dip served on the side. Two local favorites are the barbecued ribs and the catfish fiddlers, which can be enjoyed at all-you-can-eat affairs on the weekend for under $10.00. Fiddlers, those small catfish that "fiddle" with the bait of fishermen, are a local specialty that are fried whole and eaten off the bone. They, like the extra-thick catfish filets, are served with good hushpuppies and sides such as potato salad and macaroni salad or pickled beets and fries. Huge onion rings and baked beans are popular accompaniments as well.

The rough planking on the exterior creates a rustic atmosphere on the inside, where it's casual and family-friendly. Since this is the heart of tobacco country, smoking is allowed in part of the restaurant, and the friendly waitresses are efficient and attentive. Hendersonians regularly vote Ralph's the best desserts in town, and the menu features an assortment of homemade apple, pecan, chocolate, coconut and lemon icebox pies. Barbecued mutton or catfish fiddlers – whatever you order at Ralph's, you'll see why it's one of Kentucky's Fabulous Food Finds.

Rebecca Ruth Chocolate Café

1120 US 127 South
Frankfort, Kentucky 40601
(502) 875-1406

Of all the cherished confectionary creations to come from the Bluegrass, the bourbon ball comes in at the top of the list. As integral a part of any Kentucky holiday table as country ham, bourbon and benedictine, this flavorful concoction of chocolate, pecans and whiskey-spiked butter cream traces its roots back to the 1930s, when Ruth Hanly Boo came up with the process for adding bourbon to chocolate bonbons. Still a guarded secret today, her recipe for bourbon balls has become the hallmark of Frankfort's most famous candy shop, Rebecca Ruth.

Although the bourbon ball is its claim to fame, Rebecca Ruth has a lineup that will dazzle most any sweet tooth with its assortment of chocolates,

creams and candy. And in addition to that, there are now two Rebecca Ruth locations that offer a nice selection of soups, salads and sandwiches to counteract all that sugar. Soups such as creamy potato, white bean and chili are made from scratch, and sandwiches rely on staples such as pimento cheese, country ham and chicken salad for their generous fillings. Granted, it'll be difficult to keep your mind on savory dishes when you're surrounded by shelves lined with colorful candies and gleaming display cases filled with chocolate temptation, but a lunch stop at a Rebecca Ruth Chocolate Café is a must for sweet fiends and lunch buffs alike. Try this Frankfort favorite and see why I think it's one of the state's Fabulous Food Finds.

Rick's White Light Diner

114 Bridge Street
Frankfort, Kentucky 40601
(502) 330-4262

The state capital is a hotbed of local politics, but, everyone, regardless of their political stripes, seems to get along at Rick's White Light Diner. It's a tiny, unassuming place nestled up against the Singing Bridge, and to look at it you wouldn't suspect that the curmudgeon at the grill is an alum of the prestigious Culinary Institute of America. But he is. His name is Rick Paul and as a young man he had no idea he'd end up cooking for a living, much less develop a longing to run his own restaurant one day. "But," he says, "I've cooked for billionaires and statesmen, and this is the place for me."

Although the diner is something of a culinary relic and dates back to 1929 – "It's the oldest restaurant still in operation in Frankfort," says Paul – the outspoken chef has left his own mark on the eatery. Although there are only three small tables and a counter with nine stools, colorful bric-a-brac abounds, reflecting his

Don't be surprised if Rick Paul puts your food on the back burner before coming out to share his views on a variety of topics.

own quirky nature. Marilyn Monroe looks down from a poster on the ceiling, a bust of Elvis sits on the counter, a string of dried chiles hangs near the window, an old-fashioned water pump stands near the door. Not too far away is a large bass drum, rather dusty from disuse.

The menu is slightly idiosyncratic as well — one of the breakfast items is the control freak omelet — but there's a definite southern bent to it. Shrimp pie, oyster po-boys, crab cake sandwiches and Memphis-style pulled pork, courtesy of the large smoker out front, are some of the more popular items. But you'll also find burgers, grilled cheese, fish tacos, quesadillas and more, most made with organic ingredients from local producers.

Although Paul sports a cultivated sense of gruffness, it belies a soft side: people eat free on their birthdays and every ten lunches earns one free. "When you see the White Light, walk towards it." That's his advice. It's mine, too, because Rick's is one of my favorite Fabulous Food Finds in Kentucky.

If the glowing neon sign over the front window looks like a collector's item from the 1940s, that's probably because it is. So are the old cash register and scale on the front counter, and most likely the hand-lettered price lists hanging over the stainless steel sinks in the back. They even say Muhammed Ali's grandfather painted the faded "Slick Chick" mural on the wall.

In fact, you'd be hard-pressed to find anything new inside Rite Way Bar-B-Cue. The landmark has been going strong in Louisville's West End since 1943, when David Johnson opened

At only $1.25, Wesley Johnson's coney dog is a fabulous food find.

it after receiving a more than 100-year old barbecue recipe from an uncle in Tennessee.

Today, third-generation owner Wesley Johnson keeps the tradition alive, tending to the original smokers behind the pale-blue, two-story frame house six days a week. The sauce — thin compared to the thick, sweet tomato-based versions common in so many barbecue places across the country — is tangy and spicy, with the distinct sharpness of vinegar that so many barbecue aficionados say is the hallmark of true southern 'cue. And most say the ribs, with crunchy, caramelized edges and gently smoked meat tender enough to slide from the bone, are as good as any they ever ate.

Nonetheless, the pulled pork sandwich, piled high with vinegar slaw atop a generic white bun, continues to be the hottest item at Rite Way, and the $1.25 coney dog has gained a faithful following as well. Most people pop in and take their orders to go, so there's only a couple of tables inside, but don't let that stop you from sitting down and chatting with the friendly locals. It's not a fancy place, but Rite Way's been serving up good barbecue since 1943 and that's what makes it one of my Fabulous Food Finds.

Riverview Restaurant at the DuPont Lodge

Cumberland Falls State Resort Park
7351 Highway 90
Corbin, Kentucky 40701
(606) 528-4121

87.

Natural history and local beauty are specialties at the Cumberland Falls State Resort Park outside of Corbin. The centerpiece of the park is the rustic DuPont Lodge, one of many massive public works implemented during the Great Depression to employ the thousands of jobless men in Kentucky. Solid hemlock beams and knotty pine paneling complement the massive stone fireplaces in the historic hotel, which has fifty-one rooms with beautiful views and full amenities including a lodge restaurant with spectacular panoramic views of the river valley below.

Surrounded by the lush greenery and gently rolling hills of the Daniel Boone National Forest, nature lovers can sit back and enjoy a huge helping of wonderful scenery in the Riverview Restaurant. Rebuilt in 1941 after the original 1930s lodge burned, today's restaurant has enormous windows and an inviting observation deck designed to make the most of the sweeping vistas all year long.

Although many find the view the most spectacular thing on the menu, diners can fill up on down-home favorites such as hot browns and roast beef, or the lodge's famous fried catfish and hushpuppies.

Lunch at the restaurant is best followed by a brisk hike through one of the many miles of paths in the park; but dinners are especially popular several nights out of every month when the appearance of the hemisphere's only moonbow make a trek down to picturesque Cumberland Falls a romantic treat. It's the best place for a meal with a view and that's why the Riverside Restaurant at the Dupont Lodge is one of my Fabulous Food Finds.

Rosie's Restaurant

8869 East US Highway 60
Rush, Kentucky 41168
(606) 928-3547

The place isn't fancy — in fact, if there weren't cars in the parking lot, you'd probably think the place was abandoned — and the notion of second-hand smoke being dangerous apparently never crossed the minds of most of the regulars. There are rolls of paper towels at each table instead of napkins and customers often get up to refill their own coffee, however, the food at Rosie's makes a trip to Rush worth the drive. The prices are dirt cheap, the selection is impressive, and the food — home cooking served with attitude, as the waitresses will tell you — is just plain good.

Located just off Interstate 64 near the West Virginia line, Rosie's is housed in a converted gas station and serves food 24 hours a day. Breakfast is a hot item and the biscuits, large and fluffy, are especially popular. They accompany eggs served sunny side up, scrambled or over easy and they can be ordered on their own with a dozen different fillings, including country ham, sausage, bacon or tenderloin and egg. You can even treat yourself to a hot biscuit with fried bologna — now that's something you don't get every day. In addition to breakfast items, there are almost 30 sandwich selections — the Rosie burger with mushrooms and Swiss is a house specialty — and a number of sides and soups as well. The brown beans with corn bread are especially popular. Dinners come with one of 14 different main course items such as baked ham, country steak, fried chicken, fish tail or roast beef and two sides and a roll or corn

256

bread. Sides include hominy, hash browns, green beans, stewed tomatoes, and coleslaw, just to name a few. Desserts include an assortment of cakes, cobblers and raisin pie, something else you don't find on most menus anymore. I love a 24-hour place that serves raisin pie and fried bologna biscuits, so that's why Rosie's counts as one of my Fabulous Food Finds.

left: the Rosie burger; above: a nice slice of raisin pie.

Roxie's Cottage Restaurant

105 Old Porter Pike
Bowling Green, Kentucky 42103
(270) 781-4829

89

When you enter Roxie Hatler's Bowling Green restaurant, the first thing you'll notice, other than its miniscule size, is the self-serve coffee station near the front door. At Roxie's Cottage you get your own coffee. Ask the smiling senior citizen why, and she'll tell you plain and simple that she doesn't have time for that.

After another look around, the reason for this becomes clear: Roxie is a one-woman show. Taking orders, cooking, delivering food, busing tables, washing the dishes and cleaning the kitchen — she does it all, so it's good the restaurant is small. But don't let the size deceive you — there is a total of 24 seats — because on any given day Roxie will serve 100 patrons, most of them regulars and all of them there for breakfast because that's all she serves. "I used to stay open for lunch when I had a helper," she explains "but now I'm just open from 3 to 10 in the morning."

Most days when she shows up, there's already a car or two waiting for her in the parking lot. After she puts the coffee on, that's when she starts cooking up breakfast basics like pancakes, French toast, omelets and eggs anyway you like 'em. You'll also find city ham,

country ham and a grilled cheese sandwich, but Roxie is really known for her home fries and hand-made biscuits with gravy. The gravy is creamy and made from scratch and the potatoes are first boiled and sliced before going on the griddle where they get nice and crisp. The biscuits also make a nice bed for the tangy country sausage specially blended for her at nearby Kirby & Poe.

Basic as it may be, whatever you get at Roxie's will be good. That, combined with her independent spirit, makes Roxie's Cottage Restaurant one of Kentucky's Fabulous Food Finds.

Rusty Fork Café

105 South Patty Loveless Drive
Elkhorn City, Kentucky 41522
(606) 754-4494

90

When in eastern Kentucky near the Virginia border, head over to Elkhorn City for great mountain food at the Rusty Fork Café. Kathy and Johnny Stewart have run it since 1994 and it's one of those places where everyone knows everybody else and friendly waitresses like Eugenia Adkins joke with patrons as they go from table to table pouring coffee refills. Some of this playful banter with regulars has even led to several of the restaurant's signature items. One of the customers al-

ways liked his potato a certain way, so nowadays diners can enjoy a "David Earl" baked potato complete with cheese, bacon, sour cream and ham. Ask for a "cry baby" and you'll get a nice and round biscuit from the center of the pan, jazzed up with mayonnaise and bacon, just the way one demanding customer always insisted.

For a small place, the Rusty Fork has an extensive menu with over 20 sandwiches and burgers, and a wide variety of sides, for lunch. The dinner selections include spicy breaded strips of breast meat fried golden brown known as chicken planks and daily specials such as the steak and gravy with a choice of three sides. The mustard greens, brown beans and mashed potatoes are very popular, but other sides include potato salad, pickled beets, and something known as corn bread salad, a coleslaw-type blend of corn bread with kidney beans and mayonnaise.

The Rusty Fork also has a sizeable breakfast menu with a wide variety of biscuits. For a really substantial start to the day, try the special that has two eggs cooked to order with a 16-oz. steak, hash browns, fried apples and biscuits and gravy. For desserts there are local specialties like freshly baked cakes, fried apple pie, pumpkin rolls and soup beans pie, the must-have dish if you stop in. A hit with fans of pecan pie, the surprisingly delicious concoction uses nuts and coconut to camouflage the mild flavor of the legumes. You've got to love a place that's not afraid to put beans in its pie — that's why the Rusty Fork is one of eastern Kentucky's Fabulous Food Finds.

Finish off your meal at the Rusty Fork with a sweet piece of soup beans pie.

Harland Sanders Café

688 US Highway 25 West
Corbin, Kentucky 40701
(606) 528-2163

It's a museum. No, it's a restaurant. No, it's both. The very first McDonald's and the very first Pizza Hut restaurants may have ceased to exist, but the very first fast food establishment known for fried chicken is still going strong in its original location. Although most people don't go out of their way to visit your run-of-the-mill chain restaurant, this one — the birthplace of the world's most famous fried chicken — attracts fans from around the globe. Part historical museum, part culinary shrine, part fast food eatery, Harland Sanders Café pays tribute to one of the state's most well-known gastronomic exports today.

A native of Indiana, Harland Sanders moved to Corbin in 1930 and opened a service station. He operated a lunchroom with a single table surrounded by six chairs in the back of the station, but he had to expand when word spread about his good home cooking. By 1937, the future white-bearded Colonel built Sanders' Cafe, which seated 142 customers. At this restaurant, the fried chicken became the most popular selection on the menu, a fact touted by Duncan Hines in his famous travel guide. After a fire destroyed the eatery in 1939, Sanders rebuilt it as a restaurant and motel, a popular stop for travelers.

The Colonel eventually auctioned the business off and started selling franchises on his famous chicken recipe at the age of 66 and by the late 1950s, more than 200 KFC franchises had been sold in North America. John Neal, president of an 88-unit KFC franchise based in Tennessee and a great admirer of the Colonel, bought the Corbin restaurant in 1973 and refurbished it into a tourist attraction and functioning

restaurant. Aside from snagging a piece of extra crispy, today's patrons can view a variety of items from the early days of the restaurant, including the reconstructed original kitchen. It's keeping Kentucky's culinary history alive and that's why this is one of our Fabulous Food Finds today.

SANDERS CAFE

BIRTH OF A LEGEND
KENTUCKY'S
MOST FAMOUS CITIZEN

Sandstone Arches Restaurant

Natural Bridge State Resort Park
2135 Natural Bridge Road
Slade, Kentucky 40376
(606) 663-2214

Since 1889, visitors have made the trip to the mountains of eastern Kentucky to see the amazing natural wonder known as the Natural Bridge. A towering sandstone arch situated in the middle of the Daniel Boone National Forest, this geological formation became the centerpiece of a state park bearing its name in 1926. A year later, the Hemlock Lodge was built to provide guests with a comfortable place to sleep and a good meal. Although the original lodge burned, a new one constructed in 1962 on a dramatic ledge overlooking a deep valley continues its mountain hospitality today.

A 175-seat restaurant — the Sandstone Arches — capitalizes on this marvelous scenery and offers a view of famous "Hoedown Island," a one-acre piece of land in the middle of a four-acre pond that has been designated the clogging capitol of Kentucky. Although the fare features a variety of contemporary American dishes such as seared salmon with sautéed tomatoes and onions and New York strip with demi glace, the kitchen supports the Kentucky Proud program and utilizes locally grown meats and produce as much as possible.

As a result, traditional Kentucky favorites like fried catfish with hushpuppies, country ham with red-eye gravy and fried green tomatoes figure prominently on the menu. Popular items include a Kentucky Cobb salad with country ham and one of the best hot browns in the state, in addition to a hearty plate of home fries, coleslaw, sliced onion, and corn cake served with soup beans known as Kentucky country fare. For dessert, diners at Sandstone Arches often choose the chef's sweet take on apple pandowdy, a southern classic of molasses-soaked fruit baked in pastry. Give the fare at Sandstone Arches a try and see why I think it deserves to be one of my Fabulous Food Finds.

Science Hill Inn

In a state that's known for its fried chicken, it means something when people say you've got the best fried chicken around. Terry and Donna Gill, and their daughter Ellen, have been hearing this ever since they opened their restaurant at Science Hill Inn in 1978. The meat is always tender and juicy and the wonderfully light crust is crispy and flavorful, so it's hardly surprising that hungry customers have been known to drive for three hours to this old-fashioned place in downtown Shelbyville. The fried chicken stars on the regular menu that draws in a faithful clientele for both lunch and dinner, and it's also the centerpiece on the Sunday buffet, which ranks up there with the very best in the state.

Alongside the fried bird are other enticing selections such as perfectly carved slices of country ham and the most delicious, satiny, buttery mashed potatoes you'll find this side of grandma's kitchen. There are homemade salads and relishes as well, in addition to down-home favorites like cooked kale, corn pudding, and broccoli casserole. A house specialty is the deviled crab, a savory blend of crabmeat and spices baked in a cornmeal shell.

Menu favorites include Carolina shrimp served with cheese grits and bacon, Burgundy beef and noodles, and grilled shrimp and country ham skewers, which

are flavored with bourbon. Dessert selections at Science Hill reflect a preference for seasonal items and the summer months might see a tasty blueberry crisp or fresh strawberries with cream, while the decadent brown sugar pie baked in an almond crust is especially good during the colder times of year.

The Gills chose to open their restaurant in an old building that served as a girl's school from 1825 to 1939, and a sense of simplicity and decorum still pervades today. From the attentive, uniformed servers who put baskets heaped with piping hot corn bread and buttery biscuits on your table to the white-gloved grandmothers who meet their girlfriends for lunch, Science Hill Inn has preserved a slice of country elegance for all to enjoy. Science Hill Inn is without a doubt a Bluegrass classic, one of my most favorite Fabulous Food Finds of all.

Shaker Village of Pleasant Hill

3501 Lexington Road
Harrodsburg, Kentucky 40330
(800) 734-5611

The Harrodsburg area is the perfect spot to get a taste of the Shaker legacy in the Bluegrass. Founded in the early 1800s by members of the United Society of Believers in Christ's Second Appearing, the community at Pleasant Hill thrived with more than 500 residents and 4,000 acres of land by the mid 19th-century. They were a peaceful, highly innovative sect, and its adherents would come to be known as the Shakers because of their ritualistic dance.

Although the last of the Kentucky Shakers left their community at Pleasant Hill in the early 1900s, their sense of hospitality remains. Today guests at this National Historic Landmark can enjoy hearty regional

The corn pudding at Shaker Village is served family-style.

Tart and toothsome, Shaker lemon pie gets its texture and flavor from shredded lemon rind.

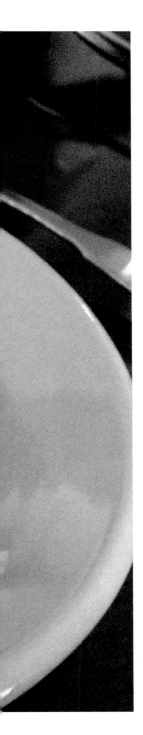

foods and original Shaker recipes at the Trustee's Office Inn, where three meals are served daily. Breakfast features a hearty country buffet with specialties such as pumpkin muffins and southern biscuits with sausage gravy, and the lunch menu offers open-faced sandwiches, salads and ham biscuits served with coleslaw and homemade corn sticks. Dinner entrées include sliced pork with apple cider sauce, rainbow trout poached in white wine, skillet-fried catfish, steak, and salt-cured country ham topped with traditional fried chicken and served with freshly baked rolls. Old-fashioned desserts such as Shaker lemon pie and chess pie are popular ways to end meals at Shaker Village. When possible, menus incorporate local ingredients and fresh seasonal vegetables grown in a historic kitchen garden.

Meals are served at Shaker Village throughout the year, however in January and February full lunch and dinner menus are offered every day in the Winter Kitchen, located in the West Family Dwelling Cellar, instead of the Trustee's Office. Dining on Shaker favorites alongside the warmth of an inviting fireplace, guests enjoy an intimate dining experience sure to help them forget the winter blahs. Whatever time of year you choose to visit, you're sure to find large helpings of history and great Shaker cooking, both things that make Pleasant Hill one of our most historic Fabulous Food Finds.

95

Shirley Mae's Café

802 South Clay Street
Louisville, Kentucky 40203
(502) 589-5295

When you plan your visit to Shirley Mae's Café, make sure you don't come during the week. That's because Shirley Mae Beard only opens her doors on the weekends. Ask her why and she'll tell you it's because it takes all week to get the food ready. "I have to process the food," she explains. "Pick the greens, the chitlins — all that stuff." And all that stuff includes cooking pig's feet, meatloaf and ribs, simmering collards, frying up chicken and making hot-water corn bread as well — all in a variety of cast-iron skillets and banged-up pots and pans.

If you're in a hurry, Shirley Mae's Café probably isn't for you because here it's all about cooking the old-fashioned southern way. You won't find fast food and mixes but rather scratch-made food "made with love," as Shirley puts it. Each piece of corn bread, for instance, is rolled individually, drawing on skills honed in the well over 20 years she's been cooking at her Smoketown location. Then it's dropped into hot oil,

Fried in hot oil, Shirley's hot-water corn bread is an old family favorite.

where it sizzles and bubbles away while she puts the rest of your order together. The result is a toothsome product with a wonderfully chewy crust and a moist interior that it is totally unlike any corn bread you've had before. And when it comes to seasonings, she relies on nothing more than salt and pepper – and, you guessed it, "a little love."

This love has brought some famous people to Shirley Mae's over the years, stars like Morgan Freeman, Whoopi Goldberg and B.B. King, but most of the faces you'll see there are regulars from the neighborhood. If they don't take their orders to go, they usually sit down and enjoy the party atmosphere in the neighborhood, because Shirley Mae's daughter Dee Simpson DJs until dawn.

Although some consider the Smoketown neighborhood a rough part of the city, Shirley Mae's proves that you can't judge a book by its cover. The company is as warm and inviting as the food, and if you can get her to take a break from peeling potatoes, cooking up ham hocks and snapping green beans, Shirley will tell you that her café is an important part of the community. In addition to helping out the hungry with free meals on Thursdays, the restaurant throws parties for children on Halloween and Christmas. "Your responsibility as a member of the community is to make the community better," says daughter Dee, and most would agree that Shirley Mae's has indeed done that. Good souls and good soul food – that's what makes Shirley Mae's a Fabulous Food Find.

Smokey Pig Bar-B-Q

2520 Louisville Road
Bowling Green, Kentucky 42101
(270) 781-1712

96

Barbecue fans zooming by Bowling Green on I-65, will want to make a quick stop at one of the area's older barbecue joints, the Smokey Pig. Located on Louisville Road, just seconds from the highway and not too far from Duncan Hines' old house, the Smokey Pig Bar-B-Q has been attracting passersby and locals alike since Phil and Kaye Huffer opened it in the early 1970s. One of its most famous guests stopped by in 2006 and garnered the old-school eatery some publicity on the national airwaves. The visitor was the Food Network's Alton Brown, and the show was the popular series *Feasting on Asphalt*.

If the name itself didn't give it away, then the swine-shaped sign towering overhead will let you know that pork is king at the Smokey Pig. You can get it in ribs, chops or shredded, in addition to main course items like chicken and hot dogs, but it's the Monroe County-style shoulder that has become its claim to fame. First, the meat is frozen and thinly sliced on a band saw; then the pork steaks are grilled over a bed of hickory coals while receiving an occasional mop of vinegary, spicy sauce. Order the shoulder plate, and they'll pile six or seven big slices one atop the other and then ask you if you want it dipped or sprinkled in the Huffer's hot vinegar sauce.

For your sides, you can opt for fluffy, buttery red skin mashed potatoes, baked beans seasoned with brown sugar and tomato and "tater" salad with mustard, bits of pimento, pickle and chives, just to name a few. The Smokey Pig is your typical low-decor barbecue place, and it's often enshrouded in a pleasant haze of wood smoke. Because their Monroe County-style barbecue has earned them a faithful following, Bowling Green's Smokey Pig is an obvious choice for our Fabulous Food Finds.

Smokey Valley Truck Stop

60 Bond Court
Olive Hill, Kentucky 41164
(606) 286-5001

Get off of I-64 at Exit 156 and drive the short distance to the Smokey Valley Truck Stop, and you'll notice something as you park your car: all the gas pumps have been removed. Owner Juanita Flaherty says she got rid of them several years ago because they were a hassle, something that turned out to be a providential move since there's more room for cars to park now. And ever since word spread about Juanita's good home cooking — especially since Guy Fieri brought the camera crew for *Diners, Drive Ins and Dives* to town in March of 2008 — the extra parking has really come in handy at this eastern Kentucky favorite.

Given that Juanita never closes her doors, she is very popular with the night owls, many of whom come in looking for a late-night breakfast. There's a good assortment of combinations with French toast, pancakes, omelets, eggs and breakfast meats, but many come specifically for the sandwiches featuring Juanita's homemade, shortening-based biscuits filled with pork tenderloin, ham, bacon or sausage. Juanita was in charge of making biscuits every morning as a young girl in boarding school and since then she's earned the unofficial title as the Biscuit Queen of Olive Hill.

In addition to breakfast items, the Smokey Valley menu offers nearly two dozen sandwiches and ten

dinners with beef, pork, chicken and fish selections, but another big draw is the list of daily specials, which include one meat item such as grilled ham steak, fried chicken breast, breaded catfish, or smoked pork chop with a choice of dinner rolls, homemade biscuits or corn bread and three different sides. In addition to turnip greens, pinto beans and potato skins, options include mashed potatoes, pickled beets, cucumber salad and whole fried potatoes.

Whatever the meal or the time of day, visitors at Smokey Valley usually make sure to save room for a piece of Juanita's famous coconut pie, a heavy custard treat spiked with vodka and topped with meringue. Give the pie and some of Juanita's other home-cooked goodies a try and discover why the Smokey Valley Truck Stop is a Fabulous Food Find.

Snug Hollow Farm Bed & Breakfast

790 McSwain Branch
Irvine, Kentucky 40336
(606) 723-4786

98

Encircled by gentle mountains and at the end of a gravel road in Estill County is the place Barbara Napier calls home, a little slice of heaven known as Snug Hollow. Among water features such as creeks and a lake, you'll find wild flowers, a log cabin, a small inn built of salvaged materials and a 300-acre working organic farm that provides much of the produce served at the acclaimed bed and breakfast inn she opened in 2001. Delicious, expertly prepared vegetarian meals, tasty lunches and country picnics, and elegant dinners featuring homemade pies and breads are the hallmark of a visit at Snug Hollow.

And then there's breakfast, of course.

"Breakfast at Snug Hollow Farm," says Napier "is served up just like the mornings, fresh, healthy and full of promise." Apart from stacks of oatmeal pancakes, savory breakfast polenta and

crispy cornmeal waffles, the first meal of the day often includes specialties such as gingered bananas, biscuits with gravy and smoked cheddar omelets, just to name a few of the early surprises. In the summer fresh fruit smoothies are also available and the cold months will see the addition of hearty dried fruit compotes and pungent cinnamon rolls to the lineup. Many of the recipes can be found in Napier's *Snug Hollow Farm Cookbook*.

Whatever the meal, the Snug Hollow experience is a feast for the eyes as well. From the artistic presentation of the plates to the rustic wooden table and idyllic views that seem to meet the eye wherever you turn, it's obvious that Barbara Napier is an artist in every sense of the word. "I consider Snug Hollow my canvas," she says, "and I love to set scenes that catch people's attention." It's this attitude, combined with a beautifully rustic setting and great vegetarian cooking, that makes Snug Hollow Farm one of Kentucky's Fabulous Food Finds indeed.

284

Fresh blackberry pie and braided rosemary bread are summertime staples at Snug Hollow.

Star Café

401 South Street
West Point, Kentucky 40177
(502) 922-4414

99

Make the trip to the sleepy hamlet of West Point less than an hour's drive from downtown Louisville, and you'll get a sample of whistle stop fare at its best. A ramshackle cluster of whitewashed buildings around the main track that slices its way through town, tiny West Point is home to one of the few remaining railroad hotels left in the country. In 1902 C. E. Hardy built an inn there to accommodate the steady stream of passengers passing through, and although the decline in rail travel caused the eventual demise of the town's hotel business, the dining room at the West Point Hotel is alive and well today.

Mary Alice Ellison and Cynthia Rutledge took over the kitchen at the Star Café in 1999 and their approach to the food they cook is best described as home cooking. Although guests can choose from a selection of salads and sandwich standards, most opt for the daily plate special for $7.50 that consists of an entrée item with two sides, and a

homemade yeast roll or corn bread. Everyday entrées include roast beef, pork tenderloin, meatloaf, and fish on Fridays and chicken on Sundays. There is a dozen sides such as stewed tomatoes, pickled beets, green beans, mashed potatoes and pinto beans to choose from and a popular plate known as the Robert Plant special offers a hearty combination of pork loin, macaroni and cheese, beans, corn bread and coffee. For dessert patrons can select almond pound cake with strawberries, German chocolate cake, buttermilk pie and banana cake with caramel icing, just to name a few. Whistle stop tradition is alive and well at the Star Café and this makes it one of 111 Fabulous Food Finds in Kentucky.

The uncomplicated concrete block construction might not attract much attention, but the iconic shade of minty green used at Starnes Barbecue makes it stand out from other buildings in the Paducah area. Well, that and the luscious, smoky barbecue that has legions of fanatics driving in from neighboring states for what many consider the best 'cue in the region — or in the country, for that matter.

Like most barbecue joints in the area, Starnes is the epitome of simplicity. Open since 1954, when Larry Starnes and his father started slow roasting meat over red-hot coals in a pit out back, it typifies the no-nonsense approach to barbecue in western Kentucky — from the preference for hickory wood down to the understated décor. There are two booths and a U-shaped counter

with a handful of stools that wraps around a soft drinks case and candy counter, and customers can order barbecue by the pound or in sandwiches.

The sandwiches are another area where Starnes stands out, because it's practically unheard of to grill a sandwich with pulled pork, sliced turkey or mutton in it. And at Starnes you can get something else in the way of sandwich fillings that you won't find at most other pit joints: barbecued bologna. Savory and slightly smoky, it's a hit with most who try it. One sauce, a tomato-based one with a bit of heat developed years ago by Larry and his father, is available at Starnes and, depending on the waitress, they'll ask if you want your sandwich "mild" (three shakes) or "hot" (six). Mild or hot—however you get your barbecue at Starnes, you'll see why it's one of Kentucky's Fabulous Food Finds.

At this Paducah institution barbecue sandwiches are grilled before serving.

290

Stinky & Coco's Diner? When Don Parsons took over a failing Winchester restaurant in December of 2009 and christened it Stinky & Coco's Diner, the name caused more than one pair of eyebrows to rise in consternation. But after locals discovered that the Chicago transplant had named the small downtown eatery after his two cats, their resolve to stay away from the oddly named locale softened and the food soon won them over. Parsons opened the place with a vision of fusing the traditional neighborhood diner or coffeehouse with something a little more quirky and modern — and the menu reflects this.

The fried egg sandwich with cheese is a hit at Don Parson's Winchester eatery.

293

Shrimp and grits — get 'em as spicy as you like at Stinky & Coco's Diner.

Aside from comfort food classics, there are some items that may not be so familiar, but whether patrons are in the mood for an old fashioned hand-formed burger or a shrimp po' boy with a spicy sriracha mayonnaise, they'll find something to like at Stink & Coco's. What they won't find, however, is a huge selection. "Instead of a big menu, we have chosen to do a few items and do them really well while mixing in daily specials," explains Parsons. "We don't do bland at Stinky & Coco's Diner either — even our sausage gravy has a kick to it."

The sausage gravy — the amount of spice can be adjusted to your personal taste, so don't be afraid to give it a try — features prominently in two of the restaurant's most popular items, the biscuits and gravy and the shrimp and grits, which can be ordered for breakfast or lunch. Other faves are the two burgers, each appropriately named after one of the cats. The Stinky Burger has a third-pound of ground chuck with lettuce, pickle, cheese, sweet onion and pickle on a buttered, toasted bun; the Coco Melt has a beef patty with melted Swiss and fried onions grilled between slices of buttered bread. Another good pick is the simple yet delicious old-fashioned sandwich that features a single fried egg with cheese and a bit of mayo on toast.

With Stinky & Coco's, Parsons not only hopes to serve up an eclectic assortment of diner fare, he also wants to create a place for people to re-connect and mingle. "Eating is a social event and personal interaction should not end after you have placed your order," he says. "I want to create a vibrant opposite to that sterile and impersonal dining experience that has become all too commonplace in our society." In addition to a catchy name, Don Parson's Winchester eatery has great shrimp and grits and an inviting proprietor — for me, that's enough to make Stinky & Coco's Diner a Fabulous Food Find.

The Tavern

1532 South Fourth Street
Louisville, Kentucky 40208
(502) 637-4200

The window signs on the unassuming brick building at the corner of Fourth and Gaulbert in Old Louisville tell you everything you need to know, their red neon letters cheerily flaunting the three main virtues of the Tavern in tiny horizontal slits: BEER. WHISKY. FOOD. For beer, you'll find the standard assortment of draft and bottle selections; for whisky, there's a lineup of good local bourbons as well as recognized labels for Irish and Canadian whisky and scotch; and for food, the fare is exactly what you'd expect for find in a neighborhood dive: fried appetizers, sandwiches, burgers, breakfast items served all day long, and the plate lunches they've been serving "since 1933."

Another sign over the front door of this quintessential hole in the wall touts their famous "Knocker Burger," a half-pound bestseller named for a previous owner, which — if the regulars know what they're talking about — will have you coming back for more. Served atop a toasted bun dressed with a bit of mayo, lettuce, tomato and a slice of cheese, this is a no-frills creation that embodies the best flavors of the classic American burger. For an introduction to the true flavors of the Tavern, try the popular lunchtime combination that pairs up the Knocker Burger and a steaming bowl of chili, a tomato-rich concoction loaded with kidney beans and lots of pleasant seasoning that is a favorite all year long.

And if you're all about hard-to-find dishes, you'll be pleased to find that the Tavern offers as a side item deviled eggs, that old-fashioned standard that most restaurants in this country scratched from the menu decades ago. At the Tavern, they're sprinkled with a little paprika just like grandma used to do, and two of them make the perfect accompaniment to the fried fish sandwich or grilled bratwurst.

In my opinion, one of the best things about the Tavern — other than the slightly grumpy waitresses and divey atmosphere, of course — is that they're "open 22 hours a day" so you know there's always an interesting late-night crowd there. It's up to you to find out which two hours they close, but if you go early enough in the morning, you're bound to run into Derek James, the man who has owned the Tavern for the last 15 years or so, and you can ask him yourself. In addition, the Tavern is located just a block from the beautiful walking court area of Belgravia Court in historic Old Louisville, one of the largest and most impressive Victorian neighborhoods in the country — that alone is enough to make it a Fabulous Food Find in my book.

Tolly-Ho Restaurant

395 South Limestone Street
Lexington, Kentucky 40508
(859) 253-2007

A compilation of the last names of founders Bob Tolley and Bob Hollopeter, Tolly-Ho Restaurant has been a 24/7 hangout at the heart of UK's campus area since 1971. Today the restaurant is in the capable hands of Roy and Sandra Milling and they are continuing the Tolly-Ho tradition of good times and good food.

Just like 30 years ago, it's a place where you can still get a cheeseburger, a big pile of fries, and soft drink for under $5. In addition to burgers, hot dogs and sandwiches, there's a wide variety of shakes and fried appetizers, not to mention oodles of breakfast items. Burgers are made with local beef that's ground fresh daily, and eggs are always cooked to order. To get an idea of why it's so popular with the student crowd, look at the menu board above the counter: a regular hamburger costs $1.09 and two eggs with toast go for $1.49.

There are two major reasons why the prices stay so low at Tolly-Ho, one of them being the fact that the owners rely on word of mouth and spend absolutely no money on advertising. The other is the hands-on approach taken by the owners, who often work the line during the late shift when students start pouring in for a much-needed study break. This is the time when you're apt to spot a group of frat boys in grass skirts or a ukulele-playing co-ed at the

No pilgrimage to UK holy ground is complete without a visit to the Tolly-Ho.

table next to you. And if you're lucky, you might witness the "initiation" of a first-timer: the person waiting on the newbie rings an extremely loud bell and announces the fact to everyone present. Because the "welcome" given by the crowd can vary in intensity depending on the time of day, make your first trip to Tolly-Ho at 3:00 in the morning and see why I think it's one of many fun Fabulous Food Finds in the Bluegrass.

299

Twig and Leaf Restaurant

2122 Bardstown Road
Louisville, Kentucky 40205
(502) 451-8944

104

One of the most identifiable landmarks along Louisville's bustling Bardstown Road — look for the flashing neon sign with the twig and leaf — this small restaurant is big on both its portions and local atmosphere. You'll find old-timers and young kids dining side by side at the counter and on any given afternoon you'll see a good blend of the people who visit and live in the neighborhood. Especially popular when late-night revelers stop by for breakfast before heading home and calling it a day, it's the Twig and Leaf, and customers have been flocking to it since 1962.

Country-fried steak sandwich

It's often crowded on the weekends, so if you don't feel like waiting for a table belly up to the counter on one of the leather stools and take a look at the menu. There are extensive offerings for all three meals, but breakfast is very popular, since you can get it anytime. Whether it's the French toast dusted with powdered sugar or the Denver scramble with green pepper, onion and ham, make sure to order the signature side dish, small pieces of fried potatoes known as Twig Taters. At lunch, the hot brown, with sliced turkey and topped with cheese sauce and bacon, is a hot item, but there are two signature items that are especially popular. One is known as Montezuma's Revenge and it consists of mounds of steaming pasta smothered with hot chili, shredded cheese, diced onion, tomato and sour cream. The other, Womb to the Tomb, is a pair of open-faced chili cheeseburgers topped with shredded letttuce, tomato and onion. Diners in search of something a bit more mainstay, say fried chicken or country fried steak, or roast beef Manhattans or club sandwiches, will be happy to find a large selection of entrée and sandwich items, in addition to the wide variety of breakfast choices. It's a late-night icon in the Louisville Highlands and that's why it's one of my Fabulous Food Finds.

Varden's

509 Main Street
Paris, Kentucky 40361
(859) 987-4700

105

Paris, the picturesque county seat of Bourbon County, is known for three things: horses, history and hospitality. Although you won't find thoroughbreds at Varden's on Main Street, you'll find a fair share of hospitality and plenty of history here. Dr. George Varden bought the current building for $2100 and completely reconstructed it to house his new pharmacy business back in 1891. The attractive façade sported pressed metal Corinthian columns embellished with rosettes, and South African mahogany apothecary cabinets accented with stained glass windows from the Tiffany Glass Company were installed to showcase the wares. Today these features still remain, and Steve Walton is keeping alive the tradition Dr. Varden started in the 19th century at his café and bistro.

In addition to salads, sandwiches are offered on the lunchtime drugstore menu, and favorites include meatloaf on sourdough, pulled pork and cole slaw on a bun, and pimento cheese with mozzarella, cheddar and asiago. For dinner, the bistro selections feature starters such as barbecue biscuits with Resting Acres ground beef and cheddar cheese and savory burgoo with braised lamb, chicken and beef with tomatoes, corn and Yukon potatoes. The entrée section has deep-fried chicken with wilted spinach and grit

cake, rack of lamb with roasted asparagus and mashed potatoes, and a fried green tomato stack for vegetarians. Bread pudding with fresh berries is a popular way to end the meal at Varden's.

There's also an emporium where you can purchase unique gift items and specialty foods from across the Bluegrass at Varden's — but stop in for a bite and discover why it's one of my 111 Fabulous Food Finds.

Wagner's Pharmacy

3113 South Fourth Street
Louisville, Kentucky 40214
(502) 375-3800

106

Located directly across from the infield gate near the corner of Fourth and Central, a popular place for lunch and breakfast with the regulars at Louisville's legendary Churchill Downs is Wagner's Pharmacy. Open since 1922, when Leo Wagner bought the store where he had worked since he was 14, Wagner's offers a true lunch-counter experience not often found these days. Aside from traditional American breakfast items, a selection of great homemade soups, burgers, and sandwiches is offered in a space decorated with racing memorabilia and old photos of Kentucky Derby winners.

One of the best parts of the Wagner's experience is the clientele; you might find yourself next to a stable hand who doesn't speak English or you may end up sharing the counter with a legendary horseman like D. Wayne Lukas or Bob Baffert. Even a Middle Eastern sheikh with his entourage has been known to walk into this low-key meeting spot that has evolved from a humble hangout for horsemen and racing writers to a favorite with the local and national media. Apart from write ups in the *Los Angeles Times* and *Southern Living*, Wagner's received great press when *The Food Network's* Bobby Flay chose its enormous Pam & Jack's Omelette as the focus of one of his famous *Throwdowns*. Loaded with green pepper, onion, tomato, ham, bacon, sausage and two different cheeses, the $8.50 house specialty has become a must-have for out-of-towners and locals alike in the whirlwind of activity that is Derby Week. This is one of the best omelets around and counts as just one reason why Wagner's joins the ranks of Fabulous Food Finds in Kentucky.

Esquire magazine named Wagner's Pharmacy one of the best places to eat breakfast in America.

Wallace Station

3854 Old Frankfort Pike
Versailles, Kentucky 40383
(859) 846-5161

Ouita Michael's Wallace Station is another culinary destination that has gotten its fair share of good press. Not too long ago Guy Fieri, television host of *Diners, Drive Ins and Dives*, stopped in at the Versailles eatery and now the entire country knows about the large portions and good food that have made it the favorite deli in Horse Country. If its picture-perfect location amidst the rolling, stone-fenced backdrop of Kentucky's premier thoroughbred farms doesn't win you over, then the racing-themed décor and huge sandwiches will.

On his visit to Wallace Station in Versailles, Fieri said the Big Brown Burger — laden with ham, bacon, tomato and cheesy Mornay sauce — counted as one of the best burgers he'd ever had. But most will tell you that the more than 20 enormously sized hot and cold sandwiches are what gained the restaurant its faithful clientele. Grilled ham and pimento cheese, shady lane chicken salad or the "inside out hot brown" with turkey, ham, bacon, tomato and white Cheddar sauce on grilled Wallace Station white — whatever you get, chances are you'll end up eating only half and having the rest wrapped up in butcher's paper to take home. They recently started serving morning sandwiches and gourmet biscuit concoctions for breakfast, so now you can enjoy the generous portions all day long. Great sandwiches and a picturesque setting put this horse country favorite high on the list of Fabulous Food Finds in Kentucky.

Weaver's Hot Dogs

131 North Main Street
London, Kentucky 40741
(606) 864-9937

108

When you've been around for over 70 years, people can assume you've been doing something right. At Weaver's, a Laurel County landmark in downtown London, what they've been doing right is hot dogs. More specifically: the chili dog — a simple beef frank nestled in a plain white bun with a draping of flavorful sauce that, over the years, has earned Weaver's something of a cult status in that part of the state.

"There's a lot of speculation about what's in our chili," says Carl David Weaver, whose grandfather opened a billiards hall on Main Street in 1940 after returning from a stint in the Army, "but I just let them keep guessing." According to family lore, Weaver Sr. bought the recipe from a traveler on his way to Mexico, and it quickly became a centerpiece on the evolving menu for hungry pool players. Although the pool tables are long gone, chili is still the main attraction at Weaver's all these years later.

The décor at Weaver's hasn't changed much, either, and scores of old black-and-white photographs line the walls, visual reminders of the town's past and its place in local history. In addition, to the left as you enter, a bank of original booths — their backs are ramrod straight and the sides are pleasantly ornate — lines the wall, the rich patina of the wood bearing witness to the decades that Weaver's has been part of the community. Because it's been around since 1940 and because the locals swear by the chili dogs, Weaver's is one of Kentucky's Fabulous Food Finds indeed.

Whistle Stop Restaurant

216 East Main Street
Glendale, Kentucky 42740
(270) 369-8586

109

The glory days of rail travel may have faded in this country, but the tradition of good food and whistle stop hospitality is still alive and well in Glendale. Just steps from the railroad track that slices its way through downtown is the Whistle Stop, a cozy eatery that opened in 1975 and quickly gained a faithful following with its down-home cooking and southern flavor. Owned by Mike and Lynn Cummins today, it's a popular small-town destination restaurant that has stayed true to its original mission of serving up affordably priced portions of simple food in a family-friendly environment.

Crack open the Whistle Stop menu and you'll find a standard selection of appetizers, soups, salads, sandwiches, steaks and main courses served with a dazzling assortment of side dishes. Some of the choices include mashed potatoes, steamed broccoli, escalloped apples, green beans, onion rings, baked potato, apple sauce, sautéed mushrooms, fried corn bread, broccoli casserole, corn pudding, lima beans and cole slaw, so if you can't find the right match to your southern-inspired dinner, it's your own fault.

Popular "main line" entrées include buttermilk-dipped fried chicken, slow-cooked pot roast, crispy catfish fingers, hand-breaded country fried steak with peppered gravy and Penn's country ham, baked and served with raisin sauce and biscuits. There's also the house favorite, savory meatloaf topped with sweet diced tomatoes, in addition to a lineup of hearty burgers.

After finishing off the meal with something sweet — try the sugar pie for something old fashioned — guests of the Whistle Stop often like to browse one of the nearby antique shops in downtown Glendale. If there's no time for shopping, make sure to pick up a copy of the *Whistle Stop Cookbook* on your way out of the restaurant. Its railroad-themed decor and family-friendly atmosphere make the Whistle Stop one of Kentucky's Fabulous Food Finds.

Wilma's

212 Court Street
Paintsville, Kentucky 41240
(606) 789-5911

110

Wilma's was a family enterprise when it opened its doors in downtown Paintsville in the 1960s and today that tradition lives on. Aside from daughters and daughters-in-law, owner Wilma Eldridge counts on several grandchildren to help operate the popular Johnson Country eatery, where homemade desserts such as the coconut cream, butterscotch, pecan and custard pies ensure a constant stream of local visitors. It was Eldridge's own mother, Granny, who helped develop the pie recipes that are still in use almost fifty years later. Wilma opens for business seven days a week and serves breakfast, lunch and dinner.

Like the pies, house-made staples such as the meatloaf and fried chicken at Wilma's are made fresh daily. Patrons can enjoy Wilma's home-style cooking à la carte or from a steam-table buffet that offers a choice of meats and assortment of sides and vegetables. Frequent stars on the buffet include roast beef, barbecue ribs, and liver and onions and the menu features items such as the Yankee Special,

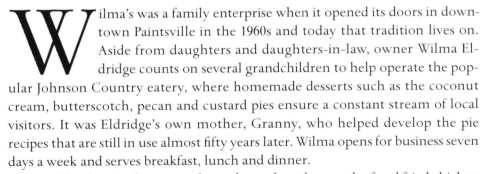

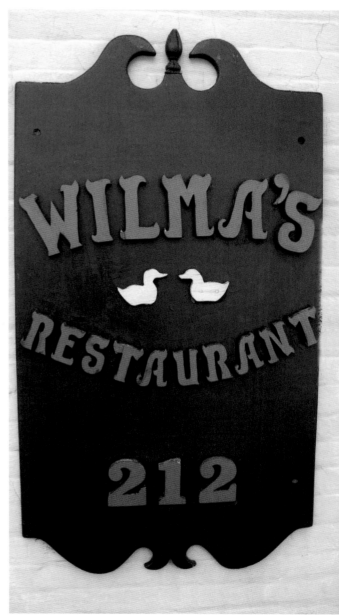

a triple-decker club sandwich with ham, turkey, bacon and cheese concocted in the days when the New York Yankees had a minor league club in town. The most enduring menu item continues to be the roast beef Manhattan, a gravy-smothered sandwich served with mashed potatoes and cole slaw.

Short on time? Wilma offers her home-cooked specials to go as well. Take-out fried chicken with buttery mashed potatoes and gravy, vegetable and a house-baked yeast roll goes for less than $5 — and that includes tax. The dirt-cheap prices and good country cooking make Wilma's one of the most Fabulous Food Finds in eastern Kentucky.

Winston's Restaurant

3101 Bardstown Road
Louisville, Kentucky 40205
(502) 456-0980

Given its credentials, it's hardly surprising that Winston's Restaurant in Louisville made the list as a 111 Fabulous Food Find in Kentucky. It is just one of a handful of select restaurants across the nation run by a team of senior gastronomical scholars, and as the final preparation for culinary graduates at Sullivan University before they enter the food-service industry as professionals, Winston's has become a popular destination for gourmands in search of innovative cooking and creative flavors.

This sleek and stylish eatery owes much of its success as a top culinary training restaurant to the well-rounded tutelage of executive chef John Castro, a longtime fixture at Sullivan's Center for Hospitality Studies who gained first-hand experience with Asian cookery while working at the Lai Lai Sheraton Hotel in Taipei, Taiwan. Over the years, Castro has developed a reputation for his cutting-edge approach to cuisine and although his menu reflects the sensibility of the Far East, it is marked by global influences and a distinct penchant for traditional Bluegrass ingredients. Bibb lettuce, hoe cakes, country ham, bourbon and chow chow are just some of the southern-inspired items that have made their way to kitchen at Winston's. "The student staff here is constantly changing," says Castro, "and our wonderful local products and a free-thinking environment provide a challenging learning experience where they can flourish and be creative."

Winston's offers lunch and brunch on the weekend, but this creativity is best sampled through a variety of small and large plates that comprise the dinner menu Friday and Saturday evenings. In addition to pavé beet salad with arugula, walnut crusted goat cheese, chopped egg and parsley vinaigrette, small plates include fried chicken livers with laughing shrimp, banana pepper tartare, spicy hollandaise and sweet chili sauce, and a popular version of the scotch egg, which is wrapped in Father's Country Ham sausage and fried in panko crumbs. For large plates diners will find options such as pork chops with sweet potato fries, southern-style kale and bourbon gastrique or herb-brined quail with pecan waffles, however a must is the mouth-watering "not brown" — a twist on the classic Louisville hot brown with fried green tomatoes, shrimp, crab, bacon, spinach and Mornay sauce.

Among its many accolades, Winston's was the first culinary school restaurant in the country invited to cook at the prestigious James Beard House in New York, and in 2007 the American Culinary Federation recognized it as the best teaching restaurant facility in the country. Stop by and see for yourself what all the fuss is about.

The menu changes often, but you might find a salad such as frisee topped with a fried egg at Winston's.

left: With juicy shrimp and crispy slices of fried green tomato, John Castro's "not brown" is a cleverly delicious contradiction of the original.

Wolf's Restaurant & Tavern

31 North Green Street
Henderson, Kentucky 42420
(270) 212-1151

and for good measure! 112

The iconic sign painted on the brick side of Wolf's Tavern in Henderson bills it as the place "where friends meet" since 1878 and today it's still a popular gathering place for family and friends in search of good food at affordable prices. It's especially crowded when UK plays, because owner Tom Davis, who is also the mayor of Henderson, reduces the drinks to half price.

Wolf's got its start when a bakery opened in the current location on May 28, 1878, but a saloon was added in the rear when George Wolf received one of the first liquor licenses in the state. Despite the unpleasantries of Prohibition, his son Frank kept the family name alive and reopened the business as a tavern in 1951. When Wolf's celebrated its hundredth anniversary in 1978, visitors received a treat: 1878 prices for many of the menu

items that had earned the small-town eatery its faithful following over the years. Although you can't get a bowl of their famous bean soup for a nickel anymore, the prices are still reasonable now that Wolf's has entered its second century of business. In addition to soup, customers will find steaks, prime rib, chicken, and sandwiches on the menu, just to name a few of the items. The company's good and the bean soup has become a staple for generations of western Kentuckians, so that's why Wolf's is the state's 112th Fabulous Food Find.

Some of my personal favorites!

Penn's Store

257 Penn's Store Road
Gravel Switch, Kentucky 40328
(859) 332-7706

Help keep them a Fabulous Food Find by going on line and making a tax-deductible donation at http://www.pennsstore.com/.

Help!

Penn's Store in Gravel Switch was all set to be one of my 111 Fabulous Food Finds until a terrible flood in May 2010 forced them to close their doors. The business has been in Jeanne Penn Lanes' family since it opened in 1850, and the rustic ceiling is still

riddled with large spike nails that once dangled the huge rolls of sausage and salt cured ham. For years, Penn's was a popular place to pop in for wonderful bologna sandwiches, which people from miles around would gobble down, but the pot-bellied stove in the middle of the floor and the walls lined with shelves of household goods and craft items represent a dying breed today. Penn's made local headlines in the 1990s when they finally added a bathroom — an outhouse — to the property, and every September, thousands commemorated the occasion by flocking to Penn's for the Great Outhouse Blowout. Sadly, that tradition — and the store's existence — is in jeopardy.

Newsom's Country Hams

208 East Main Street
Princeton, Kentucky 42445
(270) 365-2482

Visit the Ham Lady!

If you like country ham, you know who Nancy Mahaffey is. Otherwise known as the Ham Lady, her father was the famous Colonel Newsom of country ham fame. Among the finest dry-cured hams the world has to offer, Newsom's rose to national fame after the late great James Beard discovered it in 1975 and touted it in his syndicated gourmet column. Today Nancy sells the hams, along with smoked sausage, bacon, preserves, sorghum, molasses, cookbooks and other country delicacies at the store her grandfather, H.C. Newsom, established in 1917. If you can't visit her at the Old Mill Store in Princeton, go online at http://www.newsomscountryham.com/.

Two Rivers Restaurant

1608 Highway 227
Carrollton, Kentucky 41008
(502) 732-4384

Don't forget the other restaurants at Kentucky's state parks!

Many of our state parks have great restaurants. Perched on a hilltop just outside of Carrollton, where the Ohio and Kentucky rivers converge, is one of the most popular vacation destinations in the region — General Butler State Resort Park. Many guests come to camp, fish or boat, while some come for a tranquil escape in one of the comfortable lodge rooms or cozy cottages. Others come to the Butler Lodge simply for a bite to eat amidst the panoramic views of the wooded Ohio River valley. Two Rivers, the first Kentucky-themed restaurant in the state park system, combines wonderful scenery and cozy fish camp surroundings with river-inspired cuisine to produce a unique experience at breakfast, lunch or dinner. Take a trip to Two Rivers and see why it's a Fabulous Food Find. For more state park eateries, go to: http://parks.ky.gov/.

Ruth Hunt Candies

550 North Maysville Road
Mount Sterling, Kentucky 40353
(800) 927-0302

Have a sweet tooth?

At Rebecca Ruth Candies they have been making sweets since 1921. One of the most popular is the Blue Monday bar, an addictive treat of pulled cream candy covered in dark chocolate. Go online for more information at www.ruthhuntcandy.com.

323

Woodford Reserve Distillery

7855 McCracken Pike
Versailles, Kentucky 40383
(859) 879-1934

Looking for a fabulous picnic?

Visit historic Woodford Reserve Distillery from April through October and you can enjoy one of the most scenic lunches in the Bluegrass. Nestled

along Glenn's Creek with sweeping views of picturesque limestone buildings that dot the rolling countryside, the veranda at the Visitor's Center is the place to come for the yearly "picnic on the porch." You order inside and then take your lunch outside and sit down to enjoy the views. In addition to a variety of wonderful homemade sandwiches on fresh-baked bread, guests can select from an assortment of hearty soups, crisp salads, and mouth-watering pastries, pies, and sweets. If the menu seems somewhat familiar, that's because it's all put together under the watchful eye of chef-in-residence Ouita Michel, the co-owner of nearby Wallace Station and Holly Hill Inn. Woodford Reserve also offers year-round catering, so put it on your list as a future Fabulous Food Find in Kentucky.

Shuckman's Fish Co. & Smokery

3001 West Main Street
Louisville, Kentucky 40212
(502) 775-6478

Bluegrass Caviar!

Since 1919, the Shuckmans have been tempting taste palates with wonderful smoked fish products. A new addition to their lineup is caviar from spoonfish raised in Kentucky. Give them a try and see why they're turning heads. Find out more at http://www.kysmokedfish.com/

Indexed by Cities

David Dominé, otherwise known as the Bluegrass Peasant, is a shadowy figure often found lurking about the kitchens and eating establishments of whatever state he happens to be in. In addition to writing books about cooking, history, and ghosts, he enjoys traveling and searching out good places to eat. He writes a regular food column for *Kentucky Monthly* magazine and also teaches foreign languages at Bellarmine University. His previous titles include the cookbook *Splash of Bourbon: Kentucky's Spirit*, and *Ghosts of Old Louisville*, both released by McClanahan Publishing House. His current projects include Voodoo Days at La Casa Fabulosa: Memoirs of an Enchanted Neighborhood and the next installment in the *111 Fabulous Food Finds* series. If you have recommendations for fabulous food finds in your state, find him on facebook or contact him at bluegrasspeasant@insightbb.com/